THE
POWER IN
PRAISING
GOD

THE POWER IN PRAISING GOD

Charles SPURGEON

Whitaker House

Scripture quotations are taken from the *New King James Version* (NKJV),
© 1979, 1980, 1982 by Thomas Nelson, Inc. Used by permission. All
rights reserved.

THE POWER IN PRAISING GOD

ISBN: 0-88368-526-4
Printed in the United States of America
Copyright © 1998 by Whitaker House

Whitaker House
30 Hunt Valley Circle
New Kensington, PA 15068

Library of Congress Cataloging-in-Publication Data

Spurgeon, C. H. (Charles Haddon), 1834–1892.
    The power in praising God / by Charles H. Spurgeon.
        p.   cm.
    ISBN 0-88368-526-4 (pbk.)
    1. Praise of God.   I. Title.
  BV4817.S67   1998
  248.3—dc21   98-13176

    3 4 5 6 7 8 9 10 11 12 13 / 08 07 06 05 04 03 02 01 00

CONTENTS

Chapter 1

Holy Songs from Happy Saints

Now let me sing to my Well-beloved a song.
—Isaiah 5:1

A prophet inspired by God wrote these words. He did not consider singing a song of praise to be beneath his position. It was no waste of his important time to occupy himself with song. There is no activity under heaven that is more exalting than praising God. However great may be the work for which we are responsible, we will always do well if we pause to spend time in sacred praise.

I do not wish to show a preference for one spiritual exercise over another; otherwise, I think I would endorse the words of an old clergyman who said that a line of praise was even better than a page of prayer—that praise was the highest, noblest, best, most satisfying, and most healthful occupation in which a Christian could be found. If these sentiments may be regarded as the words of the church, the church of old did well to turn all her thoughts in the direction of praising God.

Though the winning of souls is a great thing, though the edifying of believers is an important matter, though the reclamation of backsliders calls for earnest attention, yet never, never, never may we cease from praising and magnifying the name of the Well Beloved. This is to be our occupation in heaven. Let us begin the music now and make a heaven of the church, even here below.

THE STRAINS OF THE SOUL'S SONG

Days without a Song

The words of the text, *"Now let me sing,"* give us a starting place. *"Now let me sing."* Does that not imply that there were times when the writer of these words could not sing? *"Now,"* said he, *"let me sing to my Well-beloved."* There were times, then, when his voice, his heart, and his circumstances were not in such a state that he could praise God.

My friends, a little while ago, we could not sing to our Well Beloved, for we did not love Him, we did not know Him, we were dead in trespasses and sins. Perhaps we joined in sacred song, but we mocked the Lord in doing so. We stood up with His people, making the same sounds as they did, but our hearts were far from Him. Let us be ashamed of those counterfeit psalms. Let us shed tears of repentance that we could so insincerely have come before the Lord Most High. Then, after being convicted of our sinful state, our guilt lay heavily on us. We still could not sing to our Well Beloved. Our music was pitched low and in a mournful minor key. We could produce only sighs and groans.

I well remember when my nights were spent in grief and my days in bitterness. A perpetual prayer, a confession of sin, and a bemoaning of myself occupied all my time. I could not sing then, and if any of you are in that condition, I know you cannot sing just now. What a mercy it is that you can pray. Bring forth the fruit that is in season, and in your case, the most seasonable fruit will be a humble acknowledgment of your sin, an earnest seeking for mercy through Christ Jesus. Take care of that, and soon, you, too, will sing a song to your Well Beloved.

Friends in Christ, it has now been a number of years since some of us first believed in Him, but since then, there have been times when we could not sing. Sad for us, there was a time when we did not watch our steps, but went astray, when the Flatterer led us from the straight road that leads to heaven and brought us into sin. Then the chastisement of God came on us. Our hearts were broken until we cried out in anguish, as David did in Psalm 51. If we did sing, we could only bring out penitential odes, but no songs. We laid aside all parts of the Psalms that had to do with praising the Lord, and we could only groan forth the notes of repentance. There were no songs for us until at last Immanuel smiled upon us once more. We were reconciled again, brought back from our wanderings, and restored to a sense of divine favor.

Besides that, we have occasionally had to sorrow through the loss of the light of God's countenance. It is not always summer weather with the best of us. Though, for the most part,

> We can read our title clear,
> To mansions in the skies.

But we have our times of fasting when the Bridegroom is not with us (Matt. 9:15). He does not intend that this world should be so much like heaven that we should be willing to stop in it; therefore, He sometimes passes a cloud before the sun so that in our darkness, we may cry out, *"Oh, that I knew where I might find Him, that I might come to His seat"* (Job 23:3).

Even the means of grace at such times will bring us no comfort. We may go to the throne of mercy in private prayer, but even there, we will perceive little light. If the Lord withdraws Himself, there is no merrymaking in the soul, but sadness, darkness, and gloom covering all. Then we hang our harps on the willows. If anyone requires a song from us, we tell them we are in a strange land, and the King has gone; how can we sing? (See Psalm 137:2–4.) Our hearts are heavy, and our sorrows are multiplied.

Also, we cannot sing the praises of our Well Beloved very well when the church of God is under a cloud. I trust we are such true patriots, such real citizens of the New Jerusalem that, when Christ's kingdom does not advance, our hearts are full of anguish. Beloved, if you happen to be a member of a divided church where the ministry appears to be without power, where there are no additions, no conversions, no spiritual life—then, indeed, you will feel that whatever the state of your own heart, you must sigh and cry for the desolations of the church of God. *"If I forget you, O Jerusalem, let my right hand forget its skill!"* (Ps. 137:5).

This is the view of every true citizen of Zion. Our hearts may flourish, and our souls may be like well-watered gardens, yet if we see the place of worship neglected, the Lord's house dishonored, the church diminished and brought low, the Gospel held in contempt, infidelity rampant, superstition stalking through the land, the old doctrines denied, and the Cross of Christ made to be of no effect, then we feel we cannot sing. Our hearts are not in tune, our fingers forget the accustomed strings, and we cannot sing a song to our Well Beloved.

With these exceptions, however, I turn to a very different strain and say that the whole life of the Christian ought to be describable by the text, *"Now let me sing to my Well-beloved a song."* From the first moment that our sin is pardoned to the last moment that we are here on earth, it should forever be our delight to sing to our Well Beloved. How can we do that? We can do it in the following ways.

Thanks-feeling

There is such a thing as "thanks-feeling"— feeling thankful. This ought to be the general, universal spirit of the Christian. Suppose you are not rich. Be thankful that you have food to eat, something to drink, and clothes to wear. Suppose that you did not have any hope of heaven. I might say to a sinner, "Be thankful that you are not in hell." But to a Christian, I would add, "Be thankful that you will never be there, and that, if just now your present joys do not overflow, yet *"there remains...a rest for the people of God"* (Heb. 4:9). Let that console you.

Is there ever a day in the year, or ever a moment in the day, in which the Christian should not be grateful? Quickly, I can respond: there is never such a day; there is never such a moment. Since we are always receiving precious blessings too numerous to count, let us continuously be exalting the hand that gives them. Before the foundation of the world, our names were engraved on the Savior's hands (Isa. 49:16). In Christ, we have always been redeemed by His precious blood, always been preserved by the power of God, always been secure of the heritage given to us in covenant by the blood of Christ; therefore, let us always be grateful. If we are not always singing with our lips, let us always be singing with our hearts.

Thanks-living

Then, we should always be "thanks-living." I think that is a better thing than thanksgiving—thanks-living. How is this to be done? By a general cheerfulness of manner, by an obedience to the command of Him by whose mercy we live, by a perpetual, constant delighting of ourselves in the Lord, and by a submission of our desires to His will. Oh, I wish that our whole life might be a psalm; that every day might be a stanza of a mighty poem; that from the day of our spiritual birth until we enter heaven, we might be pouring forth sacred music in every thought, word, and action. Let us give Him thankfulness and thanks-living.

Thanks-speaking

But then let us add "thanks-speaking." I have written often about the matter of prayer, but perhaps I should be just as earnest in addressing the matter of praise. We do not sing enough, my friends.

Do we sing as much as the birds? Yet what do birds have to sing about compared to us? Do you think we sing as much as the angels? Yet they were never redeemed by the blood of Christ. Birds of the air, will you excel me? Angels of heaven, will you exceed me? You have done so, but I intend to imitate you from now on, and day by day, night by night, I will pour forth my soul in sacred song.

Silent Thanks

We may sometimes thank God not only by feeling thankful, living thankfully, and speaking our thanks, but by silently blessing Him. This consists of suffering patiently and accepting the bad as well as the good from Jehovah's hand; it is often better thanksgiving than the noblest psalm that the tongue could express. When you bow down before Him and say, *"Not My will, but Yours, be done"* (Luke 22:42), you show Him honor equal to the "Hallelujahs" of the angels. To feel not only submitted, but willing to be anything or nothing as the Lord wills it—this is, in truth, to sing a song to our Well Beloved.

OCCASIONS WHEN WE MUST PRAISE HIM WITH SONG

When We Are Saved

The first song of praise should come when our souls realize the infinite love of Jesus for us, when we receive the pardon of sin, when we enter into the marriage relationship with Christ as our Bridegroom

and Lord. The song becomes the wedding feast.
Should it be a marriage without joyfulness? Do you
remember, even years ago, that day when you first
looked to Him and were filled with joy, when your
soul clasped His hands, and you and He were one?
Other days I have forgotten, but that day I can never
forget. Other days have mingled together unrecog-
nizably, like coins that have been in circulation so
long that their engravings are rubbed off. However,
that day when I first saw the Savior is as fresh and
distinct in all its outlines as though it were yesterday, like a newly minted coin. How can I forget it—
that first moment when Jesus told me I was His, and
my Beloved was mine (Song 6:3)?

Were any of you saved recently? Then consecrate the occasion. Pour out your soul before the
Most High. Now, if never before, let your Well Beloved receive your choicest music.

> *My heart is steadfast, O God, my heart is*
> *steadfast; I will sing and give praise. Awake,*
> *my glory! Awake, lute and harp! I will awaken*
> *the dawn.* (Ps. 57:7–8)

> *And in that day you will say: "O LORD, I will*
> *praise You; though You were angry with me,*
> *Your anger is turned away, and You comfort*
> *me."* (Isa. 12:1)

When We Come to the Lord's Table

Our first joyful days with Christ are sometimes
followed by other occasions that are not always as

joyful. Sometimes, however, we have our high days and holidays when the King entertains us at a feast. It is often like that when I come to the Communion supper every Lord's Day. I do not find that it grows stale and flat. On the contrary, I think that every time I come, I love to commemorate my Lord's sufferings in the breaking of bread better than I did before. Usually when we do come to the table, we, who know what it means, feel, *"Now let me sing to my Well-beloved a song."* It was fitting that the early disciples sang a hymn after that first Lord's Supper. We need some such expression for the sacred joy that rises in our souls at this feast.

Not only when the elements are before you, but when you hear a sermon that feeds your soul, when you read a chapter of the Bible and the promises are very precious, when you are in private prayer and are able to get very near to Jesus, I know your hearts then say, *"'Now let me sing to my Well-beloved a song.'* He has visited me, and I will praise Him. Where will my strength and rapture be spent but at His dear feet, adoring and magnifying His ever blessed name?" Oh, I wish we would often break through order and decorum to give our Lord a song. He well deserves it. May we not let cold ingratitude freeze the praises on our lips.

Now, recognizing that there are some times when we cannot sing, but that, as a rule, our life should be a praise, let us return to the text. Sometimes, on choice occasions appointed by providence and grace, our souls will be compelled to say, "Now, if never before, now beyond all other occasions, I will sing a song to my Well Beloved." I hope that all Christians will feel that way on many occasions.

Especially when you come to the table of the Lord's Supper, upon which are the emblems of your Savior's Passion, I trust you will be saying, "I feel I must sing a song to my Well Beloved, for if ever I loved Him, I love Him now."

At a Time of Deliverance

We ought to praise our Lord Jesus Christ, singing a song to our Well Beloved, particularly when we have had a remarkable deliverance. *"You shall surround me with songs of deliverance"* (Ps. 32:7), David said. Were you raised from a sickbed? Have you come through great financial difficulty? Through God's help has your character been cleared from slander? Have you been helped in some endeavor and prospered in the world? Have you seen a child restored from sickness or a beloved wife returned to you from the gates of the grave? Have you just experienced the light of Christ's countenance in your own soul? Have you been freed from a perplexing situation? Has a temptation been removed? Are you in a joyous frame of mind? *"Is anyone cheerful? Let him sing psalms"* (James 5:13). Oh, give your Well Beloved a song now when the sun is shining and the flowers are blooming. When the year turns to spring and fair weather comes, the birds seem to feel it, and they renew their music. Do the same, believer. *"For lo, the winter is past, the rain is over and gone"* (Song 2:11). Fill the earth with your songs of gratitude.

In Times of Trial

But remember, believer, you should sing songs to your Well Beloved even when troubles overtake you, when sorrows come. He *"gives songs in the night"* (Job 35:10). Perhaps there is no music so sweet as that which comes from the lips and heart of a tried believer. It is real then. When Job prospered, the Devil said, *"Does Job fear God for nothing?"* (Job 1:9). But when Job lost everything and yet said, *"The LORD gave, and the LORD has taken away; blessed be the name of the LORD"* (v. 21), then the good man shone like a star on a cloudless night. When Job blessed God, even the Devil himself could not insinuate that Job was a hypocrite. Let us be sure to praise God when things go wrong. Make certain that you sing then.

Walking one night with a companion, a holy man listened to the nightingale. He said, "Brother, that bird in the darkness is praising her Maker. Sing, I pray you, and let your Lord have a song in the night." But the other replied, "My voice is hoarse and not used to singing." "Then," said the other, "I will sing." And he sang, and the bird seemed to hear him and to sing louder still. The man sang on, and as other birds joined, the night seemed sweet with song. After a while, the good man said, "My voice fails me, but this bird's throat holds out longer than mine. I wish that I could fly away where I could sing on forever and forever."

Oh, it is blessed when we can praise God when the sun has gone down, when darkness lowers and trials multiply. Then let us say, *"Let me sing to my Well-beloved a song."* I will tell you exactly what I mean by that. You may have just passed through a very terrible trouble, and you may be almost brokenhearted. If so, you are probably inclined to say, "I will ask the prayers of the church so that I may be sustained." It is quite right, my dear one, to do that, but suppose you could be a little stronger and say, "Now I will sing to my Well Beloved a song!" Oh, it will be grand work. It will glorify God. It will strengthen you. You can say: "Yes, the dear child is dead. I cannot bring him back again, but the Lord has done it, and He always does things right. I will give Him a song, even now." "Yes, the property is gone, and I will go from wealth to poverty. But now, instead of fretfulness, I will give to my Well Beloved extra music from my heart. I will praise Him now." As Job testified, *"Though He slay me, yet will I trust Him"* (13:15). This is the part of a Christian. God help us ever to act it.

At the Time of Death

Dear friends, we may well sing to our Beloved when it is near the time of our departure. It draws near, and as it approaches, we must not dread it, but rather thank God for it. The swan is said to sing her dying song—a myth, perhaps, but the Christian, God's swan, sings sweetest at the last. Like Simeon of old, he becomes a poet at the last, pouring out his soul before God. (See Luke 2:25–35.) I hope we each desire, if we are spared to old age, to let our last days be perfumed with thanksgiving and to bless and magnify the Lord while yet we linger where mortal ears may hear the song. Break, you chains. Divide, you clouds. Be rolled up, you veil that hides the place of mystery from the world. Let our spirits pass into eternity singing. What a song to our Well Beloved will we pour out from among ten thousand times ten thousand singers (Rev. 5:11–12). We will take our part; every note will be for Him who loved us, who washed us from our sins in His own blood. Each note will be undefiled by sin; each note undistracted and undivided by worldly thoughts; each note full of perfection and acceptable to Him to whom it will be presented. Oh, long-expected day, begin! Our hearts are ready to cry out, "Open, you double doors. Let my spirit pass through the gates so that I may sing a song to my Well Beloved."

Let Everyone Bless His Holy Name

Now I will linger here a minute to address every Christian. Brother, will you sing a song for the Well Beloved? Sister, do you have a song for the Well Beloved? Aged friend, will you give Him a note? Young brother, full of vigor, will you offer a verse full of praise for Him? Oh, if we might all come to the Communion table in the spirit of praise! Perhaps some can dance before the ark like David. Others, perhaps, are on their crutches like John Bunyan's character Ready-to-halt. We read in *The Pilgrim's Progress*, though, that even he laid his crutches down when he heard the sweet music of praise. Let us bless the name of the Lord. The day has passed and been full of mercy. Evening has come. As the sun goes down, let us magnify Him whose mercy lasts through the night, will come again in the morning, and will be with us until nights and days will no more change the scene. Lift up your hearts, brothers and sisters; let every one of you lift up your hands to the name of the Most High. Magnify Him who lives forever. *"Oh, that men would give thanks to the LORD for His goodness, and for His wonderful works to the children of men!"* (Ps. 107:8).

THE QUALITY OF THE SONG

It Is a New Song

I suppose that every Christian has found that he has one of the Lord's songs to sing about. Now will I *"sing to my Well-beloved a song."* The Lord's music has one thing about it: it is always new. How very frequently we find in the New Testament that saints and angels sing *"a new song"* (Rev. 5:9). This new song is very different from the songs we used to sing, very different from the songs the world still delights in. Ours is heart-music, soul-music. Ours is real joy—no fiction. Solid joys and lasting pleasures make up the new song of the Christian. New mercies make the song always new. There is a freshness in it of which we never grow weary.

Some of you have heard the Gospel now for fifty years; has it become flat to you? The name of Jesus Christ was known to you as the most precious of all sounds fifty or sixty years ago; has it become stale now? Those of us who have known and loved Him twenty years can only say, "The more we know Him, the sweeter He is; the more we enjoy His Gospel, the more resolved we are to keep to the old-fashioned Gospel as long as we live." We could, indeed, sing a new song, though we have sung the same praises for many years.

It Is a Harmonious Song

The saints' praises have this about them: they are all harmonious. This does not mean necessarily that their voices are. Occasionally, some brother sings very earnestly through his nose, often disturbing those around him, but it does not matter how the voice sounds to the ears of man. What is important is how the heart sounds to the ears of God. If you were in a forest, and there were fifty species of birds all singing at once, you would not notice any discord. The little songsters seem to pitch their songs in keys very different from each other, yet somehow, all are in harmony.

Likewise, it is very strange that when the saints pray, they all pray in harmony. So it is when they praise God. I have attended prayer meetings where there were people from various Christian denominations. I believe the angel Gabriel would have had difficulty identifying their individual denominations when these saints were on their knees. This is the way it is with praise. I could say:

> The saints in praise appear as one
> In word and deed and mind,
> While with the Father and the Son,
> Sweet fellowship they find.

Though our words are broken and our notes fall short of the melody, if our hearts are right, our words are acceptable, and our music is harmonious to the ears of the Most High.

The Inadequacy of the Song

Beloved, notice that the saints' music always seems very insufficient to them. They feel that they must exceed the limits of earthly praise. There are some of David's psalms in which the Hebrew words are very disconnected and broken, as though the poet had strained himself beyond the power of language. How often do you find the psalmist calling on others to help him praise God? He summons not only other saints, but as if he feels their numbers are insufficient, he calls on all creatures that have breath to praise God (Ps. 150:6). How frequently do you find biblical writers invoking the dwellers above the skies, earth, air, and sea to help them lift high the praises of God? And, as if they were not content with all animated beings, you will hear them inviting the trees of the woods to break out and clap their hands while they ask the sea to roar and all of creation to magnify the Most High (1 Chron. 16:28–33).

Devout minds feel as though the whole creation is like a great organ with ten thousand times ten thousand pipes, and we little men, who have God within us, come and put our little hands on the keys and make the whole universe echo with thunders of praise to the Most High. For man is the world's priest, and the man who is blood-washed makes the whole earth his tabernacle and his temple, and every one in that temple speaks of God's glory. He lights up the stars like lamps to burn before the throne of the Most High and bids all creatures here below to become servants in the temple of the Infinite Majesty. Oh, beloved, may God cause us to be in this state of mind, and though we might think our praises are inadequate and lowly compared to the majesty of Jehovah and His boundless love, yet we will have praised Him acceptably.

It Is a Beneficial Song

I earnestly desire to encourage you to sing a song to your Well Beloved because I am quite sure the exercise will be most fitting and beneficial. Speaking for myself, I will say this: if I did not praise and bless Christ my Lord, I would deserve to have my tongue torn out of my mouth. In addition, if I did not bless and magnify His name, I would deserve to have every stone I walk on in the streets rise up and curse my ingratitude, for I am utterly in debt to the mercy of God—head over heels in debt to infinite love and boundless compassion. Are you not the same? Then I charge you by the love of Christ to awaken; awaken your hearts now to magnify His glorious name. It will do you much good, my dear ones.

There is, perhaps, no exercise that, on the whole, strengthens us as much as praising God. Sometimes, even when prayer fails, praise will encourage our hearts. It seems to prepare us for action; it pours a holy anointing oil on the head and the spirit; it gives us a joy of the Lord, which is always our strength (Neh. 8:10). Sometimes, if you begin to sing in a halfhearted mood, you can sing yourself up the ladder. Singing will often make the heart rise. The song, though at first it may appear to drag, will soon be fitted with wings that lift the spirit. Sing more, my friends, and you will sing more still, for the more you sing, the more you will be able to sing the praises of God. Singing will glorify God; it will comfort you; it will also prove attractive to those who are hesitating to become involved in the life of the church.

The melancholy of some Christians tends to repel seekers, but the holy joy of others tends to attract them. More flies will always be caught with honey than with vinegar, and more souls will be brought to Christ by your cheerfulness than by your gloominess, more by your consecrated joy than by your misery. May God help us to sing praises to Him with heart and life until we sing them in heaven. I do not doubt that we would become more useful if we praised God more, and others would join us, for they would see that God has blessed us. If God makes you feel that you must praise Him more, my purpose will have been accomplished.

I wish I could invite you all to say, "I will sing a song to my Beloved!" But there are some of you who do not love Him and cannot, therefore, sing to Him. Some years ago, I led my congregation in this hymn:

> Jesus, lover of my soul,
> Let me to Thy bosom fly.

One person present was a total stranger to the Gospel, but that touching expression, "Jesus, lover of my soul," reached his heart. He asked, "Is Jesus the lover of my soul? Then I will love Him, too." He gave his heart to Jesus and became a disciple of Christ. I pray that some who are reading this book will say the same. Then you will also sing a song to your Beloved, but first you must pray with repentance and faith. May God help you to seek and find the Savior, Jesus Christ the Lord.

Chapter 2

The Saints Blessing the Lord

Bless the LORD, O my soul;
and all that is within me,
bless His holy name!
—Psalm 103:1

Listen to David talking to himself. Earnestly, he is talking to his own soul. Every Christian should learn to soliloquize. The first audience to whom a good man ought to think of preaching is himself. Before we talk to others, we should lecture within the doors of our own hearts. Indeed, if any man desires to excite the hearts of others in any given direction, he must first stir up himself. He who would make others grateful must begin by saying, *"Bless the LORD, O my soul."* David would never have risen to the height of saying, *"Bless the LORD, you His angels"* (Ps. 103:20) or *"Bless the LORD, all His works"* (Ps. 103:22) if he had not first tuned his own voice to the joyful music.

27

PRAISE BEGINS WITH YOU

No man is fit to be a conductor of the choirs of heavenly music until he has first learned to sing the song of praise himself. *"Bless the LORD, O my soul"* is the preacher's preparation in the study, without which he will fail in the pulpit. Self-evident as this truth is, many people need to be reminded of it. They are ready to admonish others, but forget that true gratitude to God must, like charity, begin at home.

An old proverb says, "The shoemaker's wife goes barefoot." I am afraid this is too often the case in morals and religion. Preachers especially need to be watchful of themselves so that while they are motivating others to magnify the Lord, they are not shamefully silent themselves. My heart is personally warmed by the glow of thankfulness as I urge you to bless the holy name of Jehovah, our God.

But what is true of preachers is true of all other Christian workers. When they grow more earnest, the tendency among humans is to turn their passion outward, frequently in the way of faultfinding. It is wonderfully easy to become indignant at the laziness, divisions, coldness, or errors of the Christian church. We can pronounce our judgments against her, declaring her to be weighed in our balances and found lacking, as if it mattered one bit to the church what the verdict of our imperfect scales might be. Instead of writing a tract on the faults of the church, it would be easy to write a lengthy book. However, when it was completed, it would be wise to put it in the fire. Friend, pay attention to those planks in your own eye, and leave the Lord Jesus to clear the specks from the eye of His church (Matt. 7:3–4).

Begin at home. There is indoor work to be done. Instead of vainly pointing to the faults of others, earnestly praise God yourself, saying to your own heart, *"Bless the LORD, O my soul; and all that is within me, bless His holy name!"*

HOW CAN WE BLESS GOD?

Observe that the psalmist, with his audience of one, has a very choice subject: he is exhorting himself to bless God. In a certain sense, it is not possible for us to bless God. He has all things—what can we give to Him? He blesses us, and in this sense, we cannot bless Him. When we have given our best, we are compelled to confess, *"Of Your own we have given You"* (1 Chron. 29:14).

Begin with Gratitude

However, we can bless God by being thankful for the gifts He has given to us, by loving Him in response to His blessings to us, and by allowing these expressions of gratitude to influence our lives so that we speak well of His name and act in ways that glorify Him.

In these ways, we can bless God. We know that He accepts such attempts, poor and feeble though they are. God is pleased with our love and thankfulness. He is blessed by His children's desires and praises.

Bless God for Who He Is

Note that the psalmist blessed God's name, by which is meant His character. Indeed, we may take the names of God literally, for they each represent a reason to be thankful. We will praise *Jehovah*, the self-existent One. We will praise *El*, the mighty God whose power is on our side. We will praise Him who gives Himself the covenant name of *Elohim*, revealing in that name the triune nature of His sacred unity. We will praise *El Shaddai*, the all-sufficient, almighty God, and magnify Him because *"of His fullness we have all received"* (John 1:16).

Whatever other names there are in Scripture, or combination of names, will be exceedingly delightful to our hearts, and we will bless the sacred name. We will bless the Father from whose everlasting love we received our election to eternal life, the Father who has *"begotten us again to a living hope through the resurrection of Jesus Christ from the dead"* (1 Pet. 1:3). We will bless the Father of our spirits, who has given us an inheritance among all who are set apart. And we will bless the Son of God, Jesus our Savior, Christ, who has been anointed to redeem. Our hearts dance for joy at every remembrance of Him.

There is not a name of Jesus Christ's person, offices, or relationships that we should forget to bless. Whether He is Immanuel, Jesus, or the Word; whether He is Prophet, Priest, or King; whether He is Brother, Husband, or Friend—whatever name fits His beloved person is dear to us, and we will bless Him with it.

Bless God for the Holy Spirit

And the Holy Spirit, too—our Comforter, the Intercessor, the heavenly Dove, who dwells within our hearts in infinite graciousness—we will surely praise Him, too. Heaven cannot contain the Holy Spirit, yet He finds a home within the hearts of His servants. We are His temple. Each one of His influences will evoke from us grateful praise. If He is like the wind, we will be like wind chimes; if He is like dew, we will bloom with flowers; if He is a flame, we will glow with ardor. In whatever way He moves within us, we will be responsive to His voice. And while He blesses us, we will bless His holy name.

Bless God for His Character

But if the name of God is so blessed to us, certainly the character that lies beneath the name is inexpressibly delightful. Select any attribute of God, and you find a reason for loving Him. Is He unchangeable? Blessed is His name. He loves everlastingly. Is He infinite? Then glory to Him. It is endless affection that He has bestowed on us. Is He omnipotent? Then He will put forth all His power for His own beloved. Is He wise? Then He will not misjudge us or fail to bring us safely to our promised rest. Is He gracious? Then in that grace, we find our comfort and defense. Whatever there is in God, known or unknown, we will bless.

My God, I cannot comprehend You with my intellect, but I embrace You with my affections. I cannot know You fully with my mind, but I love You completely with my heart. My intellect is too narrow to contain You, but my heart expands to the infinity of Your majesty. I love You, whatever You are. You are unknown in great measure, but You are not unloved by my poor heart. Therefore, the psalmist calls on us to bless the Lord.

I would like to dwell on this emphatic phrase in the psalmist's exhortation: *"His holy name."* Only a holy man can delight in holy things. Holiness is the terror of unholy men. They love sin and consider it liberty, but holiness is slavery to them. If we are saints, we will bless God for His holiness, and be glad that in Him, there is neither spot nor flaw. He is without iniquity. Just and righteous is He. Even to save His people, He would not violate His law. Even to deliver His own beloved from going down into the pit, He would not turn away from the paths of justice. *"Holy, holy, holy, Lord God Almighty"* (Rev. 4:8) is the loftiest cry of cherubim and seraphim in their perfect bliss. It is a joyous song both to the saints on earth and those in heaven. The pure in heart gaze on divine holiness with awestruck joy.

Having briefly examined the words of our text, we will now consider the main points of the exhortation. First, it is comprehensive in its scope and calls us to bless God in the unity and diversity of our nature. Second, it shows us there are numerous attributes of praise that we must carefully consider.

BLESS GOD IN UNITY AND WITH DIVERSITY

Our first observation then will be that this exhortation is remarkably comprehensive. *"Bless the*

LORD, *O my soul"*—there is the unity of our nature; *"and all that is within me"*—there are the diverse powers and faculties that make up the variety of our nature. The unity and the diversity are both summoned to the delightful employment of magnifying God. The psalmist stirs us up to bless God with our whole being, and I pray that the Holy Spirit will help us to do this.

Bless God in the Unity of Your Nature

Bless the Lord with Your True Self

First, the unity of our nature is invited to yield its whole self to the praise of God: *"Bless the LORD, O my soul."* David praised God not only with his lips, not only with his hands on the harp strings, not just with his eyes lifted toward heaven, but also with his soul, his very self, his truest self. Never let me present to God the outward and superficial alone, but let me give to Him the inner and the sincere. Never let me bring before Him merely the outward senses that my soul uses, but the soul that uses these inner faculties. No *"whitewashed tombs"* (Matt. 23:27) will please the Lord.

"Bless the LORD, O my soul." Let my true self praise Him, the essential "I," the vital personality, the soul of my soul, the life of my life. Let me be true to the core to my God. Let that which is most truly my own vitality expend itself in blessing the Lord.

The soul is our best self. We must not merely bless the Lord with our bodies, which will become dust, but with our inner, spiritual natures, which make us like angels. Our spiritual natures are that which cause it to be said that in the image of God we were created. My spiritual nature, my loftiest powers, must magnify God—not with a voice that sings a self-righteous song of praise, but with a sincere heart; not with lips that cry "Hosanna" thoughtlessly, but with a mind that considers and intelligently worships. Not within the narrow confines of my body would I sing this song, but I would fill the limitless regions through which my spirit soars on wings of boundless thought with Jehovah's praise. My real self, my best self, will bless the Lord.

Bless the Lord with Your Immortal Self

But the soul is also our everlasting self, that which will outlast time. Being redeemed by His precious blood, it will pass through judgment and enter into the worlds unknown, forever to dwell at the right hand of God, triumphant in His eternal love. My immortal soul, why are you spending your energies upon mortal things? Will you hunt for fleeting shadows while you are most real and enduring? Will you collect bubbles, knowing that you will endure forever in a life coexistent with God Himself, for He has given you eternal life in His Son Jesus? Bless the Lord then. So noble a thing as you are should not be occupied with less worthy matters. Raise yourself, and like the angels, adore your God.

Bless God Wholeheartedly

But the words suggest yet another meaning. The soul is our active self, our vigor, our intensity. When we speak of a man throwing his soul into a thing, we mean that he does it with all his might. When we say, "There is no soul in him," we do not mean that the man does not live, but that he has no vigor or force of character, no love, no zeal. My most intense nature will bless the Lord. Not with whispered voice and restricted energy will I lisp forth His praises, but I will proclaim them vehemently and ardently in volumes of impassioned song.

Never serve God with a hand hesitant to work, which would willingly withdraw itself from labor if it could. If you do your own business in a lazy fashion, do not do God's business that way. If you go to sleep over anything, let it be over your own efforts to make money or your buying and selling. Always be awake in your service of the Lord. *"Bless the LORD, O my soul!"*

If you have ever been thoroughly awakened, awake now! If you ever were all life, all emotion, all energy, all enthusiasm, enter into the same condition again. Let every part of you be full of ardor, sensitive with emotion, nerved with impulse, borne upward by resolution, impelled by onward force. As Samson, when he smote the Philistines, used every muscle, sinew, and bone of his body in crushing his adversaries, so you should serve God with all and every force you have. *"Bless the LORD, O my soul."* O God, my hand, my tongue, my mind, my heart will all adore You:

> Every string will have its attribute to sing.
> My united, concentrated, entire being
>   will bless You,
> You infinitely glorious Jehovah!

35

Beloved, do not pretend to praise God. Praise Him with all your might. If you are a Christian, be an out-and-out Christian or let Christianity alone. Nothing hinders the glorious kingdom of Christ so much as halfhearted people, who blow hot and cold with the same breath. My friends, be thorough. Plunge into this stream of life as swimmers who dive to the very bottom and swim in the broad stream with intense delight. Do this, or else make no profession of faith.

Bless God with All Your Faculties

Use Your Heart

Then David spoke of the diverse abilities within our nature when he wrote, *"All that is within me, bless His holy name."* I think the psalm itself might indicate that, in succession, all our mental powers and passions should praise God. For instance, when he says, *"Bless the LORD, O my soul,"* he means first of all, let the heart bless Him, for that is often synonymous with the soul. The affections are to lead the way in the concert of praise.

Use Your Mind

But the psalmist intended next to arouse the memory, for he continued by saying *"forget not all His benefits"* (Ps. 103:2). May I ask you, beloved friends, to recall what God has done for you? String the jewels of His grace upon the thread of memory, and hang them around the neck of praise.

Can you count the leaves of the forest in autumn or number the grains of sand on the ocean floor? Only then could you give the sum of His loving-kindnesses. For mercies beyond count, praise Him without restraint.

Use Your Conscience

Then let your conscience praise Him, for the psalm goes on to say, *"Who forgives all your iniquities"* (v. 3). Your conscience once weighed your sins and condemned you. Now let it weigh the Lord's pardon and magnify His grace to you. Count the crimson drops of Calvary, and say, "My sins were washed away." Let your conscience praise the Sin-bearer, who has caused your mind to flow with peace like a river and to abound in righteousness like the waves of the sea (Isa. 48:18).

Use Your Emotions

Let your emotions join the sacred choir. If you are like the psalmist, you have many feelings of delight. Bless Him *"who crowns you with lovingkindness and tender mercies, who satisfies your mouth with good things, so that your youth is renewed like the eagle's"* (Ps. 103:4–5). Is all within you peaceful today? Sing some sweet verse, like the Twenty-third Psalm. Let the calm of your spirit sound forth the praises of the Lord. Do your days flow smoothly? Then consecrate your music to the Lord. Are you joyful this day? Do you feel the exhilaration of delight? Then praise the Lord with dance.

On the other hand, is there discord within? Does conflict disturb your mind? Then praise Him with the sound of the trumpet, for He will go forth with you to battle. When you return from the battle and divide the spoil, then *"praise Him with loud cymbals; praise Him with clashing cymbals!"* (Ps. 150:5). Whatever emotional state your soul is in, let it lead you to bless your Maker's holy name.

Use Your Understanding

Perhaps, however, right now your thoughts exceed your emotions. You may be considering the providence of God as you think about the histories of nations and their rise and fall. You have watched the hand of God in people's lives. So also did David, and he sang, *"The LORD executes righteousness and justice for all who are oppressed"* (Ps. 103:6). Let your judgment praise the Judge of all the earth. Let every day's newspaper give you fresh reasons for praise. Every Christian should read the paper with this intent or not at all. God's praise is the true end of history. His providence is the core of all the stories of the empires of the past. To the man of understanding, the centuries are stanzas of a divine epic where the great subject is the Lord of Hosts in His excellency.

Use Your Knowledge

Do not forget to bring your knowledge to help you in your song. You have the Scriptures, and you have the Spirit to teach you their deep insights. Therefore, you can soar above David when he sang, *"He made known His ways to Moses, His acts to the children of Israel"* (Ps. 103:7). God has made known His Son to you and in you; therefore, glorify Him.

The harvests of the fields of knowledge should be stored in the granaries of adoration. Even our human learning should be laid at the Lord's feet. We want to make each stream of knowledge increase our gratitude. Believer, do not know anything that you cannot consecrate to God, or else despise knowing it. Whatever fruits, new or old, are stored in your memory, let them all be laid up for the Beloved and none else. The censer of worship should always smoke with fragrant perfume. Knowledge should supply the spices for the incense, and love should ignite the flame.

Use Your Wonder

Be sure, too, that your faculty of wonder is used in holy things; let your astonishment bless God. If you tried to measure the distance from the east to the west, you would be lost in the immensity before you. Bless God with your wonder as you realize that your sins have been removed from you this far (Ps. 103:12). You cannot tell how high the heavens are above the earth, but let your astonishment at the greatness of creation lead you to adoration, for *"so great is His mercy toward those who fear Him"* (v. 11).

Use Your Fears

Let even your fears bow low before the Lord. Do you fear because you are frail? *"He remembers that we are dust"* (Ps. 103:14). Do you tremble at the thought of death? Then praise Him who spares you, though you are before Him like a wildflower withered by the wind as it passes over you (vv. 15–16). From a sense of your own insignificance, magnify the splendor of that gracious love that pities you, even *"as a father pities his children"* (v. 13).

Use Your Hopes

The voices of your hopes are sweet. Do not let them remain silent. As they peer into the future, let them sing: *"The mercy of the LORD is from everlasting to everlasting on those who fear Him"* (Ps. 103:17). What more could hope desire to make her raise her choicest praise? Someday, we will be where even the last verses of Psalm 103 will not be above our experience, for we will see the Lord upon the throne that He has prepared in the heavens. Then we will invite angels that *"excel in strength"* (v.20) and all the heavenly ministry to bless the Lord. How happy we are as we anticipate that day. Filled with expectation, we cry aloud, *"Bless the LORD, O my soul."*

Use Every Faculty

I think you see by now that we could look at every single mental faculty and show that David has given it room to bless God. He showed in a practical way how each individual power of the soul can praise God.

Beloved, we can no longer linger on this point. You know, each of you, what faculty you possess in the greatest strength. I pray you will use it for God. You know what attitude your soul is in just now.

Bless God while you are in that mood, whatever it may be. *"All that is within me,"* says the text—then let it be all. Some of us have a sense of humor, and though at times we try to restrain it, it sneaks out. What then? Let us allow even this faculty to be under the Lord's control. It is not necessarily common or coarse. Let it be used for the Lord.

On the other hand, some of you have a touch of melancholy in your nature. Take care to bring it under subjection in praising the Lord. You are the ones to sing those serious melodies, which in some respects are the pearls of song. A little thoughtfulness is good flavoring. Music is at its best when it is pleasingly melancholic.

Use Your Uniqueness

Praise God, my beloved, as you are. Larks do not refrain from singing because they are not nightingales. The sparrow does not refuse to chirp because it cannot imitate the finch. Let every tree of the Lord's planting praise the Lord. Clap your hands, you trees of the woods, while fruitful trees and all cedars join in His praise (Ps. 148:9). Both young men and women, the aged and children, praise the name of the Lord. Each one adds his distinct note, and all are important in making perfect harmony.

The Lord would not want you to borrow your brother's tones, but to use *"all that is within [you],"* all that is individual to your character, for His glory. Spend all your strength, yes, every atom of it. Keep back nothing, but give *"all that is within [you]"* to Him. If everything within you is the Lord's, all that is on the outside of you that is yours will also be His. All your bodily faculties will praise Him, and your inner and outer life will be all for God.

Use Your Possessions

Let your house praise Him. Beneath its roof may there ever be an altar to the God of all. Let your table praise Him. Learn to eat and drink to His glory. Let your bed praise Him. Let the very clothes that you wear, seeing they are gifts of His love, remind you to praise the Lord. Each breath you breathe should inspire a new song to the Preserver of all. Make your life a psalm, and be yourself an incarnate hymn: *"all that is within me, bless His holy name!"*

THE QUALITIES OF PRAISE

Now let us consider what the text reveals about the characteristics of praise and the manner in which we are to praise God.

Praise Is Reasonable

First, the suggestion of the text is sensible. God has created all that is within us except the sin that mars us. All of our faculties, receptivity, powers, and passions are of the Lord's fashioning. We would not be able to feel, to think, to hope, to judge, to fear, to trust, to know, or to imagine if He had not granted us the power. Who should own the house but the builder? Who should have the harvest but the farmer? Who should receive the obedience of the child but the father? To whom, then, O my soul, should you give respect but to Him who made you all that you are?

Moreover, the Lord has redeemed our entire being. When mankind had gone astray, and all our faculties, like lost sheep, had taken their own roads of sin, Christ came into the world and redeemed our entire nature—spirit, soul, and body—not a part of us, but our complete humanity. Jesus Christ did not die for our souls only, but for our bodies, too. Though at present *"the body is dead because of sin,"* and therefore we suffer pain and disease, yet *"the Spirit is life because of righteousness,"* and *"if Christ is in* [us],*"* we have a sure guarantee that He *"will also give life to* [our] *mortal bodies"* (Rom. 8:10–11). We will, at the coming of the Lord, be wholly restored in body and soul by the Lord's divine power. Therefore, let body and soul praise Him who has redeemed both by His most precious blood.

Your body is not yours to pamper; you are to serve the Lord, for His blood has paid your ransom and secured your resurrection. Your soul, your spirit, whatever faculty you have, Christ's blood covers all; therefore, you are not your own. It would be sad, indeed, even to think of having an unredeemed will or an unredeemed judgment. But it is not so. Every faculty is freed by His ransom. If the blood on the lintel and doorposts has saved the house (Exod. 12:23), then it has saved every room, and every part of our lives should be consecrated to the Redeemer's praise.

Beloved, the Lord has given innumerable blessings to every part of our nature. I wrote of these faculties in the previous section, one by one. It would be very easy to show that all our faculties are the recipients of blessing. Therefore, they should all bless God in return. Every pipe of the organ should yield its quota of sound. As an eagle's every bone, muscle, and feather is made with a view to flight, so is every part of a regenerate man created for praise. As all the rivers run into the sea, so all our powers should flow toward the Lord's praise.

To prove that this is reasonable, let me ask one question: if we do not devote all that is within us to the glory of God, which part is it that we should leave unconsecrated? And the part that is less consecrated to God, what should we do with it? It would be impossible to give a proper answer to this question. An unconsecrated part in a believer's human nature would become a nest of hornets or a den of devils, out of which devils would come to prowl over our entire being. An unsanctified faculty would be a leprous spot, a valley of misery, a Dead Sea, a den of pestilence. To be sanctified, spirit, soul, and body (1 Thess. 5:23), is essential to us, and we must have it; it is but our *"reasonable service"* (Rom. 12:1). *"All that is within* [us]*"* must bless God's holy name. To withhold part of the price is robbery; to reserve part of our territory from our King is treason.

Praise Is Necessary

I not only insist that praise is reasonable, but also that it is required. It is necessary that the whole nature bless God, for at its best, when all parts are engaged in the service of praise, it still

44

fails to complete the work, falling short of the praise Jehovah is due. All humans, with all their might, always occupied in all ways in blessing God, would still be no more than a whisper in comparison with the thunder of praise that the Lord deserves. One of our poets expressed it aptly when he wrote:

> But, ah! eternity's too short
> To utter all Thy praise.

Praise Him Fully

It is true. All of God's creatures would be incapable of reflecting the whole of divine glory. The mercy and grace God shows to us in the gift of His dear Son is so great that the church militant on earth and the church triumphant in heaven together are not capable of offering sufficient praise. Let us not, therefore, insult the Lord with half when the whole is not enough. Let us not bring Him the tithe, when, if we had ten times as much, we could not magnify Him as we should.

We must, moreover, give the Lord all because divided powers in every case lead to failure. Those who have succeeded in anything have almost always concentrated on one thing. He who is a jack-of-all-trades is a master of none. He who can do a little of this and a little of that never does much of any one thing. The fact is that there is enough water in the stream of our being to turn only one waterwheel, and if we divide it into many trickling brooks, we will accomplish nothing. The right thing to do is to dam up all of our forces and allow them to expend themselves in one direction. Then we can pour them all forth upon the constantly revolving wheel of praise to God. How can we afford to let life evaporate in trifles when one aim only is worthy of our immortal being?

We who have been baptized by profession of faith were taught in that solemn ceremony to bless the Lord with our entire being. We were not sprinkled randomly, but by the outward sign, we were *"buried with Him through baptism into death"* (Rom. 6:4). We were immersed into the name of the triune God. If our baptism meant anything, it declared that from that point on, we were dead to the world. We owned no life but that which came to us by way of the resurrection of Jesus. As the water flowed over our heads, we surrendered our minds with all their powers of thought to Jesus. Over the heart, the veins, the hands, the feet, the eyes, the ears, the mouth, the significant element poured itself, symbol of that universal consecration that floods all the inward nature of every sanctified believer. I charge you who have been baptized, do not corrupt your profession of faith.

All or Nothing at All

Remember, beloved, this one striking point: Jesus Christ will have all of us or nothing. He will have us sincere, earnest, and intense, or He will not have us at all. I see the Master at the table. His servants place before Him various meats so that He may eat and be satisfied. He tastes the cold meats, and He eats the bread hot from the oven. As for tepid drinks and half-baked cakes, He pushes them away with disgust. To those who are cold and are mourning their coldness, He will give heat. He will look on those who are hot, who serve Him with the best they have. But to the man in the middle, the lukewarm, He says, *"I will vomit you out of My mouth"* (Rev. 3:16). Jesus cannot bear lukewarm religion; He is sick of it.

Much of the religion of this present time is nauseating to the Savior rather than acceptable. *"If the LORD is God, follow Him; but if Baal, follow him"* (1 Kings 18:21). Let there be no mockery, but be true to the core. Be thorough; throw your soul into your religion. I charge you to stand back awhile and count the cost. If you wish to give Christ a little and Baal a little, you will be cast away and utterly rejected—the Lord of heaven will have nothing to do with you. *"Bless the LORD,"* then, *"all that is within me,"* for only such sincere and undivided honor can be accepted by the Lord.

Wholehearted Praise Is Beneficial

I now ask you to give your attention to the next observation: sincere praise is good for us. To be wholehearted in the praise of God elevates our faculties. There can be no doubt that many a person's powers have been debased by the object being pursued. Poets who might have been great poets have missed the highest seats of honor because they have selected trivial topics or impure themes. Therefore, the best features of their poetry have never been fully developed. *"Bless the LORD,"* and you will be a person who reaches your fullest capacity. This is the way to reach the loftiest peak of human attainment.

Praise Promotes Spiritual Growth

Consecration cultivates our spiritual development. To praise is to learn. To bless God is also useful to us in terms of preventing self-centeredness. We cannot bless God and at the same time idolize ourselves. Praise preserves us from being envious of others, for by blessing God for all we have, we learn to bless God for what other people have. I consider it to be a great part of praise to be thankful to God for making better men than I.

If we are always blessing the Lord, we will be saved from complaining; the spirit of discontent will be ejected by the spirit of thankfulness. This will also deliver us from laziness, for if all our powers magnify the Most High, we will scorn the soft couch of ease and seek the place of service in order to bring more honor to our Master.

Praise Is Becoming

Nothing beautifies a person like praising God. To plunge our whole nature in adoration adorns the spirit. I was told by one who experienced the revivals in Northern Ireland years ago that he never saw the human face look so lovely as when it was lit up with the joy of the Holy Spirit during those times of refreshing.

You know how pleasing landscapes appear when the sun shines on them. The scenery has not half its charms until the sun of this great world enriches the view with its wealth of color, making all things glow with glory. Praise is the sunlight of life. Beneath a cloud of indifference, some of you conceal all the beauty of your character. You are like the lovely mountains in the Lake District of Cumbria. When they are enshrouded in mist, little or nothing is visible.

Like a heavenly wind, may grace drive away the fog of despondency and discontent and shed the sunlight of true praise all over our souls. Then the beauty of our new creation will be observed. May we have many lovely praising Christians abounding in our world.

Praise Is Good for Others

While wholehearted praise is beneficial to us, it is also useful to others. I am persuaded that many souls are converted by the cheerful conversation of Christians. Many already converted are greatly strengthened by the holy joy of their brothers and sisters in the Lord. You cannot do more effective good than by living a happy, consecrated life spent in blessing God. Do not think that contemplation is the fairest flower of piety. Some prominent Christians appear to resemble Christ in the sorrow that marred His face rather than in the joy that sustained His spirit.

Jesus sorrowed so that we might rejoice. It is truly Christlike to *"rejoice in the Lord always"* (Phil. 4:4). We should seek to have Christ's joy fulfilled in ourselves. If anything is cheerful, joyous, glistening bright, full of heaven, it is the life of a man who blesses God all his days. This is the way to win souls. We will not catch flies with vinegar. We must use honey. We will not bring men into the church by displaying black crepe and shrouds in the windows of our churches while standing silently at the door like funeral directors. No, we must tell the truth and show sinners the best robe, the wedding ring, and the silver sandals of joy and gladness. We must sing:

> The men of grace have found
> Glory began below;
> Celestial truths on earthly ground
> From faith and hope do grow.

In Thomas Cooper's *Plain Talk*, I read a story of a Sunday school teacher who was in a sad state of mind. He announced a somber hymn for the class to sing:

> Ah, whither should I go
> Burden'd, and sick, and faint.

No one seemed too inclined to sing, so the leader asked a certain fellow named Martin to start a song. "No, no," said Martin. "I'm neither burdened, nor sick, nor faint. I'll start no tune, not I!"

"Well, then, Brother Martin," said the leader, "pick out a song you like." So with all the power of his lungs, Martin sang:

> Oh for a thousand tongues to sing
> My great Redeemer's praise.

That is the hymn, my friend. Keep to that. If you do not have a thousand tongues, at least let the one you have continue to bless the Lord while you have any breath.

Praise Prepares Us for Heaven

Finally, all this praise is preparatory. If we can strive for constant praise now, it will get us ready for all that lies ahead. We do not know what will happen to us between now and heaven, but we can easily predict the final result. We are harps that will be tuned for the concerts of the blessed. The Tuner is putting us in order. He sweeps His hands along the strings. There is a discord from every note, so He begins first with one string, and then moves to another. He stays at each string until He hears the exact pitch.

The last time you were ill, one of your strings was tuned. The last time you had a bad debt or trembled at declining business, another string was tuned. And so, between now and heaven, you will have every string set in order. You will not enter heaven until all are in tune.

Have you ever gone to a place where they make pianos and expected to hear sweet music? The tuning room is enough to drive a person mad. In the factory, you hear the screeching of saws and the noise of hammers, and you say, "I thought this was a place where they make pianos." Yes, so it is, but it is not the place where they play them.

Earth is the place where God makes musical instruments and tunes them. Between now and heaven, He will put all that is within them into proper condition for blessing and praising His name eternally. In heaven, every part of our being will bless God without any difficulty. There will be no need for a preacher to exhort you. There will be no need for you to talk to yourself and say, *"Bless the LORD, O my soul."* You will do it as naturally as you now breathe. You never give any consideration as to how often you breathe, nor do you have any plan laid down as to when your blood will circulate. These matters come naturally to you. In heaven, it will be your nature to praise God. You will breathe praise. You will live in an atmosphere of adoration. Like those angels who for many ages, day without night, have circled the throne of Jehovah rejoicing, so will you. But I will not write much on that, or you will be wanting to fly away to our own dear country—

> Where we will see His face,
> And never, never sin;
> But from the rivers of His grace
> Drink endless pleasures in.

You must stay a little longer in the tents of Kedar and mingle with the men of soul-distressing Meshech (Ps. 120:5). When daybreak comes and the shadows flee away, say to your soul, *"Bless the LORD, O my soul; and all that is within me, bless His holy name."*

For Those Who Cannot Praise

I wish all my readers could, but some of you cannot bless God at all. It would be useless for me to tell you to do it. You are dead in your sin. I read a story the other day of a woman convinced of her sinful state by a single dream. She dreamed that she saw her minister standing in the middle of a number of flowerpots that he was watering. She thought that she was one of the flowerpots, but the minister passed her by, and said, "It is no use watering that plant, for it is dead. I must pass by the dead plants."

Oh, sinner, can you bear this? I cannot invite you to sing the believer's song of praise. Can you bear to be left out? Though I pass you by, I pray the Lord will look at you, and say, "Live!"

Before I close, I must tell you something else, which is meant for dead sinners as well as for living saints. It is this: *"Believe on the Lord Jesus Christ, and you will be saved"* (Acts 16:31). God grant to you that saving faith for Christ's sake.

Chapter 3

Prayer Perfumed with Praise

*In everything by prayer and supplication,
with thanksgiving, let your requests
be made known to God.*
—Philippians 4:6

According to the text, we are to make our requests known to God both by prayer and supplication. If any distinction is intended here, I suppose that by prayer is meant the general act of devotion and the mention of our usual needs. By supplication, I think would be intended our distinct entreaties and special petitions. We are to offer the general prayer common to all the saints, and we are to add to it the special and definite petitions that are unique to us. We are to worship in prayer, for God is to be adored by all His saints. Then we are to request His attention for our own needs, according to the words of the text, letting God know our requests.

Do not forget this second form of worship. There is a good deal of generalizing in prayer. God forbid that we should say a word against it, insofar as it is sincere worship, but we need to have more definite pleading with God, asking Him for specific things with a clear knowledge of what we ask. You will hear prayers at prayer meetings in which everything is asked in general but nothing in particular. Yet the reality and heartiness of prayer will often be best displayed by requests for distinct blessings.

See how Abraham, when he went to worship the Lord, did not merely adore Him, and in general pray for His glory, but on a special occasion, he pleaded concerning the promised heir (Gen. 15:2–6). Another time he cried, *"Oh, that Ishmael might live before You"* (Gen. 17:18). On one special occasion, he interceded for Sodom. (See Genesis 18:20–33.)

Elijah, when on top of Mount Carmel, did not pray for all the blessings of God in general, but for rain, for rain then and there. He knew what he was driving at, kept to his point, and prevailed. (See 1 Kings 18:36–37.)

My beloved friends, we have many needs that are so burdensome. As they weigh on us heavily, they become very distinct and definite. We ought to have just as many clearly defined petitions that we humbly ask God to answer. We should watch with eager expectancy for His divine response, so that when we receive His answer, we may magnify our Lord.

COMBINING PRAYER AND PRAISE

This is the point I want to make: whether we are praying a general prayer or asking for a specific need to be met, we are to offer both requests *"with thanksgiving.*" We are to pray about everything, and every prayer should be blended with praise. Since we are to pray without ceasing (1 Thess. 5:17), it follows that we should always be in a thankful condition of heart. Since we are not to pray without thanksgiving, it is clear that we should always be ready to give thanks to the Lord. We must say with the psalmist, *"Thus I will bless You while I live; I will lift up my hands in Your name"* (Ps. 63:4). The constant tenor and spirit of our lives should be adoring gratitude, love, reverence, and thanksgiving to the Most High.

This blending of thanks with devotion is always to be maintained. We must offer *"prayer and supplication, with thanksgiving."* Even if the prayer struggles out of the depths, its wings should be silvered with thanksgiving. Even if a prayer is offered by someone who is on the verge of death, in the last few words his trembling lips can utter, there should be notes of gratitude mixed with the words of petition.

The law instructed that *"with all your offerings you shall offer salt"* (Lev. 2:13). The Gospel states that all your prayers should be offered with praise (Phil. 4:6). "One thing at a time" is considered to be a wise proverb, but in this case, I must risk contradicting it. Two things at a time are better when the two are prayer and thanksgiving. These two holy streams flow from one common source: the Spirit of life that dwells within us. They are expressions of the same holy fellowship with God; therefore, it is right that they should mingle as they flow and find expression in the same holy exercise.

Supplication and thanksgiving so naturally run into each other that it would be difficult to keep them separate. Like kindred colors, their shades run into each other. Our very language seems to indicate this closeness, for there is little difference between the phrases "to pray" and "to praise." A psalm may be either a prayer or praise or both. There is another form of utterance, which is certainly prayer, but is used as praise and is really both. I refer to that joyous Hebrew word that has been imported into numerous languages: *Hosanna*. Is it a prayer? Yes, it means: "Save, Lord." Is it praise? Yes, for it is tantamount to "God save the king" and is used to extol the Son of David.

While we are here on earth, we should never attempt to make a distinction between prayer and praise. We should neither praise without prayer nor pray without praise. But with every prayer and supplication, we should mingle thanksgiving as we make our requests known to God.

This commingling of precious things is admirable. It reminds me of that verse in which the king is described as coming from the wilderness in his chariot *"like pillars of smoke, perfumed with myrrh and frankincense, with all the merchant's fragrant powders"* (Song 3:6). There is the myrrh of prayer and the frankincense of praise. In ancient Israel, the holy incense of the temple sanctuary yielded the smoke of prayer, which filled the Holy Place. With it, there was the sweet perfume of choice spices, which may be compared to praise. Prayer and praise are like the two cherubim on the ark of the covenant. They must never be separated.

In the model of prayer our Savior has given us, the opening part is praise rather than prayer: *"Our*

Father in heaven, hallowed be Your name" (Matt. 6:9). The closing part of it is praise: *"For Yours is the kingdom and the power and the glory forever. Amen"* (v. 13).

The Example of David

David, who is the great tutor and example of the church as to her worship, being at once her poet and preacher, took care in almost every psalm, though the petition was agonizing, to mingle exquisite praise. For instance, in the psalm written after his great sin with Bathsheba, one would think that he might have almost forgotten or have feared to offer thanksgiving while he was trembling with sighs and groans and tears under a great sense of wrath; yet before the psalm that begins *"Have mercy upon me, O God"* can come to a conclusion, the psalmist has said: *"O Lord, open my lips, and my mouth shall show forth Your praise"* (Ps. 51:15). He could not pen the last word without beseeching the Lord to build the walls of Jerusalem, adding the promise, *"Then You shall be pleased with the sacrifices of righteousness, with burnt offering and whole burnt offering; then they shall offer bulls on Your altar"* (v. 19).

I do not need to quote other instances, but it was almost always the case that David warmed himself into praise by the fire of prayer. He began with many broken notes of complaining, but he mounted and glowed and, like the lark, sang as he ascended. When at first his harp was muffled, he warbled a few mournful notes. Then he became excited until he could not restrain his hand from that well-known and accustomed string reserved for the music of praise alone.

There is a passage in which he seemed to have caught the very idea that I want you to focus on: *"I will call upon the LORD, who is worthy to be praised; so shall I be saved from my enemies"* (Ps. 18:3). He was in such a condition that he said, *"The pangs of death surrounded me, and the floods of ungodliness made me afraid. The sorrows of Sheol surrounded me; the snares of death confronted me"* (vv. 4–5).

Driven by distress, he declared that he would call upon the Lord; that is, he would pray. But he did not regard God only as the hearer of his prayer, but as One who is deserving of his praise: *"I will call upon the LORD, who is worthy to be praised"* (v. 3). Then, as if inspired to inform us that the blending of thanksgiving with prayer makes prayer infallibly effective, he added, *"So shall I be saved from my enemies"* (v. 3).

THE EXAMPLE OF PAUL

If this habit of combining thanksgiving with prayer is found in the Old Testament saints, we have a right to expect it even more in the New Testament believers, who in clearer light perceive fresh reasons for thanksgiving. I will use Paul as an example. He told us that those things that we have seen in him, we are to do (Phil. 4:9), for his life was in harmony with his teachings.

Notice how frequently he began his letters with a mixture of supplication and thanksgiving. Look at Romans 1, and you will see this fusion of precious metals:

> *First, I thank my God through Jesus Christ for you all, that your faith is spoken of throughout the whole world. For God is my witness, whom I serve with my spirit in the gospel of His Son, that without ceasing I make mention of you always in my prayers.*
>
> (Rom. 1:8–9)

Here we find both *"I thank my God"* and *"I make mention of you always in my prayers."* This was not purposefully written to correspond to the intention of our text; it was natural for Paul to thank God when he prayed.

Look at Colossians 1:3: *"We give thanks to the God and Father of our Lord Jesus Christ, praying always for you."* To the same effect, we read in 1 Thessalonians 1:2: *"We give thanks to God always for you all, making mention of you in our prayers."* Look also at 2 Timothy 1:3: *"I thank God, whom I serve with a pure conscience, as my forefathers did, as without ceasing I remember you in my prayers night and day."* And since it is so in other epistles, we are not at all surprised to find a mixture of prayer and praise in Philippians 1:3–4: *"I thank my God upon every remembrance of you, always in every prayer of mine making request for you all with joy."*

It is noteworthy in itself (and those to whom Paul wrote must have remembered the incident) that in Philippi, Paul and Silas prayed and sang praises to God at midnight so that the prisoners heard them. It is clear that Paul habitually practiced what he here preached in our text. His own prayers were not offered without thanksgiving.

61

With this as an introduction, I invite you to consider carefully and prayerfully, the grounds of thanksgiving in prayer, the evil of its absence, and the result of its presence.

THE BASIS FOR THANKSGIVING IN PRAYER

There are reasons for mingling thanksgiving with prayer. We have abundant cause, my friends, for being thankful at all times. We do not come to God in prayer as if He had left us absolutely penniless, crying to Him like starving prisoners begging through prison bars. We do not ask as if we had never received a single cent from God before and doubt that we will receive anything now. On the contrary, having already been the recipients of immense favors, we come to a God who abounds in loving-kindness, who is willing to shower good gifts on us and waits to be gracious to us. We do not come to the Lord as slaves to an unfeeling tyrant, craving a blessing. Instead, we come as children who approach their loving Father, expecting to receive abundantly from His liberal hands. Thanksgiving is the right spirit in which to come before the God *"who daily loads us with benefits"* (Ps. 68:19). Think for a while what reasons you have to be thankful in prayer.

Prayer Is Possible

First of all, be thankful that such a thing as prayer is possible. That a finite creature can speak with the infinite Creator, that a sinful being can have an audience with the infinitely holy Jehovah is astounding. It is worthy of thanksgiving that God commanded prayer and encouraged us to draw near to Him. Moreover, it is amazing that He should have supplied all the things necessary to practice the sacred exercise. He has set up a blood-sprinkled mercy seat. He has prepared a High Priest, who *"always lives to make intercession for* [us]*"* (Heb. 7:25). To these, He has added the Holy Spirit, who *"helps in our weaknesses. For we do not know what we should pray for as we ought, but the Spirit Himself makes intercession for us"* (Rom. 8:26). Everything is ready, and God waits for us to come to Him with our requests.

He has not only set before us an open door and invited us to enter, but He has given us the right spirit with which to approach. The grace of supplication is poured out upon us and worked in us by the Holy Spirit. What a blessing it is that we do not attempt prayer by chance, as if we were trying a questionable experiment. Nor do we come before God hopeless, desperately afraid that He will not listen to our cry. But He has ordained prayer to be the regular business of heaven and earth and sanctioned it in the most solemn manner. Prayer may climb to heaven, for God has Himself prepared the ladder and set it down before us. At the top of that ladder is the Lord Himself in His covenant capacity, receiving our petitions and sending His attendant angels with answers to our requests. Will we not bless God for this?

Prayer Is Permissible

Let us praise His name, dear friends, especially since you and I are still spared to pray and permitted to pray. What if we are greatly afflicted? We should be glad that because of the Lord's mercy, we are not consumed (Lam. 3:22). If we had received our due, we would not have been on praying ground and pleading terms with Him. It is for our comfort and to God's praise that we can still stand with bowed head and cry, *"God, be merciful to me a sinner!"* (Luke 18:13). We are free to cry out like sinking Peter, *"Lord, save me"* (Matt. 14:30). Like David when he was fleeing from Saul, we may be unable to go to the temple, but we can still go to God in prayer. The Prodigal has lost his wealth, but he has not lost his power to ask for restoration. Although he has been feeding pigs, he is still a man who has not lost his senses. Temporarily, he may have forgotten his father, but his father has not forgotten him. He may get up and return to his father. He may pour out his soul to his father's heart. Therefore, let us thank God that He has never said to us: "Seek my face in vain" (Isa. 45:19).

If we find a desire to pray trembling within our souls, if we feel some hope in the promise of our gracious God even though that hope is almost extinct, if our hearts still groan after holiness and after God even though they have lost their power to pray with joyful confidence as they once did, yet let us be thankful that we can pray, even if it is but a little. In the will and power to pray lies the capacity for infinite blessedness: the one who has the key of prayer can open heaven. Yes, he has access to the heart of God. Therefore, bless God for prayer.

Prayer Is Reasonable

Beyond the fact of prayer and our power to exercise it, there is a further ground for thanksgiving in that we have already received great mercy at

God's hands. We are not coming to God to ask favors and receive them for the first time in our lives. Why, blessed be His name, if He never granted me another request, I have enough for which to thank Him as long as I have any being. Remember this: whatever great things we are about to ask, we cannot possibly be seeking for blessings one-half so great as those we have already received if we are indeed His children. If you are a Christian, you have life in Christ. Are you about to ask for food and clothes? Life is more than these. You have already obtained Christ Jesus. He who did not spare Him will not deny you anything. Is there anything to compare with the infinite riches that are already ours in Christ Jesus?

Let us perpetually thank our Benefactor for what we have while we are requesting something more. Should it not be so? The memory of His great goodnesses runs over into our requests until our petitions are baptized in gratitude. While we come before God empty-handed to receive of His goodness, we should never appear before Him empty, but come with the fat of our sacrifices, offering praise and glorifying God.

Prayer with Acceptance Is Triumphant

Furthermore, when we come before God in the hour of trouble, remembering His great goodness to us in the past and therefore thanking Him, we ought to have enough faith to believe that the present trouble, about which we are praying, is sent in love. You will win with God in prayer if you can look at your trials in this light: "Lord, I have this thorn in the flesh (2 Cor. 12:7). I beg You to deliver me from it, but meanwhile I bless You for it. Although I do not understand the why or the wherefore of it, I am persuaded there is love within it. Therefore, while I ask You to remove it because it seems painful to me, if it may to Your better knowledge work to my good, I bless You for it. I am content to endure it as long as You see fit."

Is that not a sweet way of praying? "Lord, I am in need. Please answer my request. Meanwhile, if You do not, I believe it is better for me to be in need, and so I praise You for my necessity while I ask You to supply it. I glory in my infirmity (2 Cor. 12:9) even while I ask You to overcome it. I triumph before You in my affliction, blessing You for it even while I ask You to help me through it and rescue me out of it." This is a royal way of praying. Such a combination of prayer and thanksgiving is more precious than gold.

Prayer Works

Furthermore, beloved, when we are on our knees in prayer, we should bless God that our prayers have been answered so many times before. We should say, "Here Your poor petitioner bends before You to ask again, but before he asks, he thanks You for having heard him so many times before. I know that You hear me always (John 11:42), therefore I continue to cry to You. My praises urge me to make fresh petitions, encouraging me in the full confidence that You will not send me away empty-handed." Why, many of the mercies that you possess and rejoice in today are answers to prayer. They are dear to you because, like Samuel, whom his mother so named because he was "asked of God," they came to you as answers to your earnest requests.

When mercies come in answer to prayer, they have a double delight about them, not only because they are good in themselves, but because they are certificates of our favor with the Lord. Well, then, since God has heard us so often and we have the proof of His hearing, should we ever grumble and complain while we pray? Should we not rather feel an intense delight when we approach the throne of grace, a rapture awakened by sunny memories of the past?

Prayer Develops Our Faith

We should pray with complete thanksgiving because God has given us the mercy we seek. I wish we could learn this high virtue of faith. In talking with my dear friend George Müller, I have frequently been astonished at the way in which he mentions that he has for so many months and years asked for a specific request and praised the Lord for its answer. He praises the Lord for it as though he has actually obtained it. Even in praying for the conversion of a person, as soon as he has begun to intercede, he also begins to praise God for the conversion of that person. Though I think he told me that he has been praying thirty years for a certain request, and the answer has not yet been received, still all the while he continues to thank God because he knows the prayer will be answered. He believes that he has his petition and begins to magnify the Giver of it.

Is this unreasonable? How often do we thank people for actions that they have not yet accomplished? For example, if you were to promise some poor person that you would pay his rent when it came due, he would thank you directly, though not a cent had left your pocket. We have enough faith in our fellowmen to thank them beforehand, so surely we can do the same with our Lord. Should we not be willing to trust God for a few months or even for years if His wisdom asks us to wait? This is the way to win with Him. The Scripture says, *"Whatever things you ask when you pray, believe that you receive them, and you will have them"* (Mark 11:24).

As a man's promissory note stands for his pledge to repay the money, so let God's promise be accounted as the performance. Will heaven's banknotes not pass as cash? Yes, truly, they will have unquestioned acceptance as currency among believers. We will bless the Lord for giving us what we have sought in accordance with His will since our having it is a matter of absolute certainty. We will never thank God by faith and then find that we were fooled. He has said, *"Whatever things you ask in prayer, believing, you will receive"* (Matt. 21:22). Therefore, we can rest assured that the thanksgiving of faith will never bring shame to the face of the man who offers it.

Surely, friends, if the Lord does not answer the prayer we are offering in the way that we desire, He is still so good, so supremely good. Therefore, we will bless Him whether or not He answers in the way we have requested. We should praise Him when He does not answer us and bless Him for refusing our desires. How devoutly might some of us thank Him

that He did not answer our prayers when we sought
for harmful things in the ignorance of our childish
minds. If we asked for meat, He might have sent us
quails in His anger. (See Numbers 11:4–6, 18–23,
31–34.) While the meat was yet in our mouths, His
wrath might have come upon us. But in love, He
would not hear us. Blessed be His name for closing
His ear in pity! Let us adore Him when He keeps us
waiting at His doors, thank Him for denials, and
bless Him for refusals, believing always that Ralph
Erskine spoke the truth when he said:

> I'm heard when answered soon or late,
> Yea, heard when I no answer get:
> Yea, kindly answered when refused,
> And treated well when harshly used.

Faith glorifies the love of God, for it knows that
the Lord's roughest usage is only love in disguise.
We are not so low-down as to make our songs or
praise depend upon the weather or the quantity of
our blessings. Blessed be His name. He must be right
even when He seems at cross purposes with His people. We are not going to quarrel with Him like silly
children with their babysitters because He does not
happen to grant us every desire of our foolish hearts.
Though He slay us, we will trust in Him even if He
declines our requests (Job 13:15).

We ask Him for our daily bread, and if He with-
holds it, we will praise Him. Our praises are not de-
pendent upon His answers to our prayers. As the
prophet wrote:

> *Though the fig tree may not blossom, nor fruit
> be on the vines; though the labor of the olive*

*may fail, and the fields yield no food; though
the flock may be cut off from the fold, and
there be no herd in the stalls; yet I will rejoice
in the LORD, I will joy in the God of my salvation.*   (Hab. 3:17–18)

This is the sum of what I have said: under every
condition, and in every need, draw near to God in
prayer, but always bring thanksgiving with you. As
Joseph said to his brothers, *"You shall not see my
face unless your brother is with you"* (Gen. 43:3),
may the Lord say to you, "You will not receive My
smile unless you bring thankfulness with you."

Let your prayers be like those ancient manu-
scripts that one sometimes sees, in which the initial
letters of the prayers are gilded and adorned with
multiple colors, the work of masterful artists. Let
even the general confession of sin and the litany of
mournful petitions have at least one illuminated letter. Light up your prayers with rays of thanksgiving
all the way through. When you come together to
pray, do not forget to speak *"to one another in
psalms and hymns and spiritual songs, singing and
making melody in your heart to the Lord"* (Eph.
5:19).

THE PERILS OF PRAYING WITHOUT PRAISE

Second, I will try to show the evil of the absence
of thanksgiving in our prayers.

Ingratitude

First and foremost, if we pray without praising,
we should be charged with ingratitude. Are we always

to be receiving and never returning thanks? Aristotle rightly observes: "A return is required to preserve friendship between two persons." As we have nothing else to give to God except gratitude, let us give it abundantly. If we have no fruit of the field, let us at least give to God the fruit of our lips. Have we no thanks to bring? How, then, can we expect further blessings? Does not generosity itself close its hand when ingratitude stands in the way? What, never a word of gratitude to Him from whom all blessings flow!

Selfishness

Next, it would indicate great selfishness if we did not combine praise with prayer. Can it be right to think only of ourselves, to pray for benefits and never honor our Benefactor? Are we going to bring the hateful sin of greed into spiritual things and care only for our own soul's good? What, no thought for God's glory? No idea of magnifying His great and blessed name? May God prevent us from having such mean, greedy spirits. Healthy praise and thanksgiving must be cultivated because they prevent prayer from becoming overgrown with the mildew of selfishness.

Lack of Faith

Thanksgiving also prevents prayer from becoming an exhibition of a lack of faith. Some prayer shows the absence of faith rather than the exercise of confidence in God. When I am in trouble, if I still bless the Lord for all I suffer, my faith is seen. Before I obtain mercy, if I thank God for the grace that I have yet to taste, my faith is shown.

Is our faith such that it sings only in the sunshine? Have we no nightingale music for our God? Is our trust like the swallow, which leaves us in winter? Is our faith a fragile flower that needs a greenhouse to keep it alive? Can it blossom like the gentian at the foot of a frozen glacier, where the damp and chill of adversity surround it? I trust it can. It should. We ought to be able to praise and bless God when outward circumstances would cause us to sigh rather than to sing.

Willfulness

Not to thank God in our prayers would demonstrate willfulness and lack of submission to His will. Must everything happen according to our plans? To refuse to praise unless we have our own way is great presumption. It shows that like a naughty child, we will sulk if we cannot be master. It is like the little boy who was very diligent in saying his prayers, but was at the same time disobedient, ill-tempered, and pesky. His mother told him that she thought it was hypocritical for him to pretend to pray. He replied, "No, Mother, indeed it is not. I am praying that God will lead you and Daddy to like my ways better than you do."

Numbers of people want the Lord to "like their ways better," but they do not intend to follow the ways of the Lord. Their minds are contrary to God and will not submit to His will. Therefore, there is no thanksgiving in them. Praise in a prayer is indicative of a humble, submissive, obedient spirit. When it is absent, we may suspect willfulness and self-seeking. Much of the prayer of rebellious hearts is the mere growling of an angry stubbornness, the whine of an ungratified ego. God must do this and He must do that or else we will not love Him. What baby talk! What spoiled children! A little correction will do them good.

I knew a good man whose child was on the verge of death. When I went to see her, he instructed me not to mention death to her. He said, "I do not believe God could do such an unkind thing as to take my only child away." When I assured him that it was likely that she would die in a few days and that he must not quarrel with the will of the Lord, he stood firm in his rebellion. He prayed, but he could not bless God. It was no surprise that his heart sank within him, and he refused to be comforted when at last his child did die. Afterwards, he became resigned, but his reluctant submission cost him much pain.

This will not do. This quarreling with God is not good. Acceptance comes to the heart like an angel in disguise, and when we entertain it, our souls are comforted. We may ask for the child's life to be spared, but we must also thank the Lord that the dear life has been prolonged as long as it has. We must put the child and everything else into our Father's hands, and say, "Lord, even if You take all away, I will still bless Your name, O Most High." This is an acceptable prayer because it is not soured by the leaven of self-will, but salted with thankfulness.

Discord

We must mingle thanksgiving with our prayers; otherwise, we may find that our minds are not in harmony with the divine will. Dear friends, the purpose of prayer is not to try to change the mind of God. Prayer is the shadow of the laws of the Eternal. God has ordained His plans, and He molds His saints to will what He wills and to express their desires in prayer. Prayer is the rustling of the wings of the angels who are bringing the blessing to us.

It is written, *"Delight yourself also in the LORD, and He shall give you the desires of your heart"* (Ps. 37:4). It is not promised that He will give everyone the desires of his heart. First, you must delight in the Lord. When your mind finds all its joy in God, then it is clear that God and you, as much as can be, are standing on the same plane and moving in the same direction. Then you will have the desire of your heart because the desire of your heart is the desire of God's heart.

Powerlessness

Character, as much as faith, lies at the basis of persistence in prayer. I do not mean in the case of the prayer of the sinner when he is seeking mercy, but I mean in the habitual prayers of the godly. Some men cannot pray with strength enough to triumph because sin has made them weak. God walks contrary to them because they walk contrary to Him. He who has lost the light of God's countenance has also lost much of the power of his prayers. You do not suppose that every Israelite could have gone to the top of Mount Carmel and opened the windows of heaven as Elijah did. No, he must first be Elijah, for it is the *"effective, fervent prayer of a righteous man"* that *"avails much"* (James 5:16). When the Lord has put your heart into agreement with His, then you will pray and prevail. Our Lord said, *"If you abide in Me, and My words abide in you, you will ask what you desire, and it shall be done for you"* (John 15:7).

Without a doubt, many lose power in prayer because their lives are deplorable in the sight of the Lord, and He cannot smile upon them. Will any father listen to the requests of a child who has set himself up in opposition to parental authority? The obedient, tender, loving child, who would not wish for anything that you did not think was right to give, is he whose requests you are pleased to consider and fulfill. You even anticipate the wishes of such a child before he asks. May we be this type of children of the great God.

THE REWARDS OF THANKFUL PRAYER

Praise Produces Peace

In the third place, let us consider the result of the presence of thanksgiving in connection with prayer. According to our text, thanksgiving blended with prayer produces peace:

> *In everything by prayer and supplication, with thanksgiving, let your requests be made known to God; and the peace of God, which surpasses all understanding, will guard your hearts and minds through Christ Jesus.* (Phil. 4:6–7)

That peace, that conscious calm, that divine serenity, which is described as the peace of God, is not produced by prayer alone, but by prayer with thanksgiving. Some men pray, and that is commendable. But because their prayers lack praise, praying disturbs them. They come away more anxious than when they started. If their requests were mingled with praise, like chemists who expertly mix compounds in just the right proportions, the blessing of God would flow from their prayers, resulting in rest for the heart.

If we bless our gracious Lord for the specific troubles we are praying about, if we bless Him for the mercy that we need as if it had already come, if we resolve to praise Him whether we receive the answer or not, learning to be content in spite of our circumstances (Phil. 4:11), then *"the peace of God, which surpasses all understanding, will guard* [our] *hearts and minds through Christ Jesus"* (Phil. 4:7). Beloved, if you value this divine rest of spirit, if you prize constant serenity of soul, I beg you to mingle praises with your prayers.

Praise Releases Prayer

In addition to bringing peace, thanksgiving often warms the soul, enabling it to pray. I believe it is the experience of many who cherish their devotional time to encounter periods when they cannot pray. Their hearts seem hard, cold, silent, and almost dead. Do not work at creating unwilling and formal prayer, my friends. Instead, take down the hymnal and sing. While you praise the Lord for what you have, you will find your stony hearts beginning to soften. You will be encouraged to enter into the presence of the Lord because you will remember what you have already received from His hand.

If you had to raise an empty wagon to the mouth of a coal pit, it might be a very difficult task for you. But the work is managed easily by the common sense of the miners. As the full wagons run down, they pull the empty wagons up the incline. Likewise, when your heart is loaded with praise for mercy received, let it run down the incline and draw up the empty wagon of your desires. Then you will find it easier to pray. If our hearts can be warmed and renewed by so simple a method as asking the Lord to accept our thanksgiving, let us by all means take care to use it.

Praise Precedes Victory

Finally, I believe that when a man begins to pray with thanksgiving, he is on the edge of receiving the blessing. God's time to bless you has come when you begin to praise Him as well as pray to Him. God has His set time to answer us, and He will not grant our desires until the proper season has arrived. However, the time has come for you to bless the Lord.

Look at this example from 2 Chronicles 20:20–22. Jehoshaphat went out to fight a massive army, and notice how he achieved the victory.

So they rose early in the morning and went out into the Wilderness of Tekoa; and as they went out, Jehoshaphat stood and said, "Hear me, O

> *Judah and you inhabitants of Jerusalem: be-*
> *lieve in the LORD your God, and you shall be*
> *established; believe His prophets, and you*
> *shall prosper."* And when he had consulted
> with the people, he appointed—

What? Warriors? Captains? No, that was already
done, but he appointed—

> *those who should sing to the LORD, and who*
> *should praise the beauty of holiness, as they*
> *went out before the army and were saying:*
> *"Praise the LORD, for His mercy endures for-*
> *ever." Now when they began to sing and to*
> *praise, the LORD set ambushes against the*
> *people of Ammom, Moab, and Mount Seir, who*
> *had come against Judah; and they were de-*
> *feated.*

Victory came when they began to sing and
praise. Your answer to prayer will come when you
multiply your thanksgiving in all your prayers. Be
assured of that.

Our thanksgiving will show that the reason for
our waiting is now over. The waiting has answered
its purpose and may now come to a joyful end. Sometimes we are not in a proper state to receive a
blessing, but when we reach the condition of thankfulness, then is the time when it is safe for God to
bless us.

A professing Christian came to his minister once
and said, "Sir, you say we should always pray." "Yes,
my friend, undoubtedly." "But I have been praying
for twelve months to enjoy the comforts of religion,

and I am no happier than before. I have made that my one perpetual prayer, and I do not feel joy or even peace of mind. In fact, I have more doubts and fears than I ever had before." "Yes," said his minister, "and that is the natural result of such a selfish prayer. Why, dear friend, come and kneel down with me, and let us pray in another manner: 'Father, glorify Your name. Your kingdom come.' Now, go and offer those petitions and get to work to try to make them true. See if you do not soon enjoy the comforts of religion."

There is a great truth here: if you will desire that God be glorified and aim at glorifying Him yourself, then the joys of true godliness will come to you in answer to prayer.

The time for the blessing is when you begin to praise God for it. For, dear ones, you may be sure that when you offer thanksgiving on the grounds that God has answered your prayer, you really have prevailed with God.

Suppose you had promised some poor woman that you would give her a meal tomorrow. You might forget it, you know. But suppose when the morning came, she sent her little girl with a basket for it. She would be likely to get it, I think. Suppose that, in addition, she sent a little note thanking you in advance for your great kindness. Would you have the heart to say, "My dear girl, I cannot pay attention to you today. Come another time"? Oh, no. If your cupboards were bare, you would go out to get something. You would find a way to meet her need because the good soul believed in you so much that she had sent you thanks for the food before she even received your gift.

Well, now, trust the Lord in the same manner. He cannot go back on His Word. Believing prayer holds Him, but believing thanksgiving binds Him. Even evil people will fulfill a pledge when they know that a thankful person is counting on them. How much more will our good God answer the prayers of a thankful heart? You can depend on God. The time for receiving is at hand because thanksgiving for the gift not yet received fills your heart. It is up to you. If you are able to pray with gratitude, great good will come to you, to the church of God, and to the world at large.

Someone reading these words may feel, "I cannot pray like that. I do not know how to pray. Oh, I wish I knew how to pray! I am a poor, guilty sinner. I cannot mix any thanksgiving with my requests."

Dear soul, do not think about that just now. These words I have written are more for the people of God. Your prayer should be a simple one: *"God, be merciful to me a sinner"* (Luke 18:13). And yet, I would venture to say that there is praise even in that prayer. You are implicitly praising the justice of God and praising His mercy by appealing to Him. When the Prodigal returned, he began his plea by saying, *"Father, I have sinned against heaven and in your sight, and am no longer worthy to be called your son"* (Luke 15:21). In that confession was a real praise of the father's goodness, which the son felt unworthy to receive.

First, you have to find Jesus and eternal life in Him. Go and plead the merit of Jesus. Cast yourself upon the love and mercy of God; He will not cast you away. Then, after you have found Him and know Him, take care that you never stop thanking Him for the gift of your salvation. No matter what circumstances life brings you—hunger, poverty, and need or health and wealth—continue to bless your saving Lord, saying, *"This poor man cried out, and the LORD heard him"* (Ps. 34:6), and *"I will sing to the LORD as long as I live; I will sing praise to my God while I have my being"* (Ps. 104:33). God bless you for Jesus' sake.

Chapter 4

Praise God

For of Him and through Him and to Him
are all things, to whom be glory forever. Amen.
—Romans 11:36

My text consists almost entirely of simple words, but it contains the loftiest of thoughts. Such tremendous meaning is concentrated here that an archangel's eloquence would fail to convey its glorious teaching. Not even angels could grasp its full impact. I can truly say that no man living can preach a sermon worthy of this text. Among all the sacred orators and eloquent preachers, none ever lived nor will any live who would be capable of reaching the height of the great argument contained in this verse.

I utterly despair of successfully describing the greatness of God; therefore, I will not even attempt to explain the infinite glory contained in this verse. Only our great God can explain this Scripture, for He alone knows Himself, and He alone can worthily proclaim His own perfection. Yet I am comforted by the thought that in answer to our prayers, God will speak from this text to our hearts, if not through the words of the writer, then through His own still small voice to which the believer's ear is so well tuned. If He will bend down to bless us, our hearts will be lifted.

Two things are presented to us in the text: doctrine and devotion. The first one is worthy of our observation, the second of our imitation. The doctrine is high doctrine—*"Of Him and through Him and to Him are all things."* The devotion is lofty devotion—*"To whom be glory forever. Amen."*

THE DOCTRINE

Let us consider the doctrine. The apostle Paul explains the general principle that all things come from God: they are of Him as their source; they are through Him as their means; they are to Him as their end. They are of Him in the plan, through Him in the working, and to Him in the glory that they produce. Taking this general principle, you will find it applies to all things, and it is our job to see those examples where it is most obvious. May the Lord, by His Holy Spirit, open His treasures to us at this moment so that we may be enriched in spiritual knowledge and understanding.

God Alone

Meditate, dear friends, upon the whole range of God's works in creation and providence. There was a time when God dwelt alone, and creatures did not exist. In that time before all time, when there was no day but the Ancient of Days, when matter and created mind were alike unborn, and even space was not, God, the great I AM, was as perfect, glorious, and blessed as He is now. There was no sun, yet Jehovah dwelt in indescribable light. There was no earth, yet His throne stood fast and firm. There were no heavens, yet His glory was unbounded. God inhabited eternity in the infinite majesty and happiness of His self-contained greatness.

The Divine Counselor

If the Lord, abiding in this majestic solitude, chose to create anything, the first thought and idea had to come from Him, for there were no others to think or suggest. All things had to be of Him in design. From whom could He receive counsel? Who could instruct Him? No others existed to give Him counsel, even if such an assistance could be imaginable. In the beginning of His way, before His works of old, eternal wisdom brought forth from its own mind the perfect plan of future creations. The creative design was clearly the Lord's alone.

The Master Designer

He ordained the pathway of every planet and the place of every fixed star. He created the *"cluster of the Pleiades,"* and bound Orion with his belt (Job 38:31). He appointed the boundary of the sea and settled the course of the winds. As to the earth, the Lord alone planned its foundations and shaped its design. In His own mind, He formed the mold of all His creatures and found for them a home and a purpose. He appointed the degree of strength with which He would endow each creature, settled its months of life, its hour of death, its comings and goings. Divine wisdom mapped this earth, its flowing rivers and foaming seas, its towering mountains and laughing valleys. The divine Architect fixed the gates of the morning and the doors of the shadow of death. Nothing could have been suggested by any other, for there was no other to suggest. It was in His power to create a universe very different from this one if He had so pleased; He must have made it what it is because in His wisdom and prudence He saw fit to do so.

The All-Knowing Sovereign

He could have created a world from which sin could have been forever excluded. That He permitted sin to enter into His creation must again be attributed to His own infinite sovereignty. If He had not known with certainty that He would be Master over sin and that out of evil would evolve the noblest display of His own glory, He would not have permitted it to enter the world. However, in sketching the whole history of the universe that He was about to create, He permitted even that black spot to defile His work. He knew in advance what songs of everlasting triumph would rise to Him when in streams of His own blood, incarnate Deity would wash out the stain of sin. It cannot be doubted that whatever may be the whole drama of history in creation and providence, there is a high and mysterious sense in which it is all of God. The sin is not God's, but the temporary permission of its existence formed part of the foreknown scheme. Neither the interference of evil in the moral nature of man nor the purity of God's divine character diminishes the force of our belief that the whole scope of history is of God in the fullest sense.

The Supreme Creator

When the plan was all laid down, and the Almighty had ordered His purpose, this was not enough: mere arrangement would not create *"through Him"* as well as *"of Him."* He had to create the universe out of nothing. He did not call for help—He does not need it, and besides, there is none to help Him. There was no raw material that He could fashion between His palms and launch forth as stars. He did not need a mine of unquarried matter to melt and purify in the furnace of His power before skillfully hammering it out upon the anvil. No, there was nothing to begin with in that day of Jehovah's work. From the womb of Omnipotence, all things must be born.

He speaks, and the heavens leap into existence. He speaks again, and worlds are created with all the varied forms of life so filled with divine wisdom and matchless skill. *"'Let there be light'; and there was light"* (Gen. 1:3) was not the only time God spoke into existence things that were not. He also spoke forth the rolling earth and blue heavens, which blossomed out of nothingness. *"Through Him"* were all things, from the high archangel who sings His praises in celestial notes to the cricket chirping on the hearth. The same finger paints the rainbow and the wings of the butterfly. He who dyes the garments of evening in all the colors of heaven has

covered the king's cup with gold and lit the glow-
worm's lamp. From distant, massive mountains that
pierce the clouds down to that minute grain of ocean
sand—all things are made *"through Him."* If God
were to withdraw the radiance of His divine power,
everything would melt away as the foam upon the
sea melts into the wave that bore it. Nothing could
stand an instant if the divine foundation were removed. If He should shake the pillars of the world,
the whole temple of creation would fall to ruin, and
its very dust would be blown away. A dreary waste, a
silent emptiness, a voiceless wilderness is all that
would remain if God were to withdraw His power;
no, nothing would remain if His power were removed.

The Omnipresent God

Nature exists through the energy of the omnipresent God. If the sun rises every morning and the
moon walks in her brightness at night, it is *"through
Him."* Away with those men who think that God has
wound up the world as though it were a clock and
has gone away, leaving it to work for itself apart
from His present hand.

God is present everywhere—not just when we
tremble because His thunder shakes the solid earth
or He sets the heavens in a blaze with lightning. He
is present in the calm summer's eve when the air so
gently fans the flowers, and gnats dance up and
down in the last gleams of sunlight.

Men try to forget the divine presence by calling
His energy by strange names. They speak of the
power of gravitation, but what is that? We know

what it does, but what is it? Gravitation is God's own power. They tell us of the laws of electricity and other scientific data. We know the laws, and let them wear the names they have, but laws cannot operate without power. What is the force of nature? It is a constant issuing from the great Fountain of power, a constant flowing out of God Himself, the perpetual radiance of light from Him who is the great *"Father of lights, with whom there is no variation or shadow of turning"* (James 1:17).

Tread softly. Be reverent, for God is here as truly as He is in heaven. Wherever you are, and whatever you see, you are in God's workshop, where every wheel is turned by His hand. Everything is not God, but God is in everything. Nothing works, or even exists, except by His present power and might. *"Of Him and through Him...are all things."*

Creation Praises the Creator

Beloved, the greatest glory of all is that in the work of creation everything is *"to Him."* Everything will praise the Lord: He so designed it. God must have the highest motive, and there can be no higher motive conceivable than His own glory. When there was no creature but Himself, and no being but Himself, God could not have taken His motive from a creature that did not exist. His motive must be His own. His own glory is His highest aim. Carefully, He considers the good of His creatures, but even the good of His creatures is but a means to the main end, the promotion of His glory. All things then are for His pleasure, and for His glory they daily work.

Tell me that the world is marred by sin, and I lament it. Tell me that the slime of the Serpent is upon everything beautiful here, and I sorrow over it. But yet, even yet, will everything speak of the glory of God. *"To Him are all things,"* and the day will come when we will see, with spiritually illuminated eyes, that even the introduction of the Fall and the Curse did not mar the splendor and majesty of the Most High. *"To Him"* will all things be. His enemies will bow their heads unwillingly but abjectly, while His people, redeemed from death and hell, will cheerfully praise Him. The new heavens and the new earth will ring with His praise, and we who will sit down to read the record of His creating wonders will say of them all, *"Glory!"* (Ps. 29:9).

The Victorious One

Courage, then, beloved, when you think that matters go against the cause of God. Rest on His sovereignty like you would relax upon a soft couch. When the Enemy hisses in your ears, "God is overcome. His plans are spoiled. His Gospel is thrust back. The honor of His Son is stained," tell the Enemy, "No, it is not so; *'to Him are all things.'"* God's defeats are victories *"because the foolishness of God is wiser than men, and the weakness of God is stronger than men"* (1 Cor. 1:25). In the end, we will see most clearly that it is so. Hallelujah!

We will see, dear friends, one day in the clear light of heaven, that every page in human history, however stained by human sin, has nevertheless something of God's glory in it. The calamities of nations, the falling of dynasties, the devastation of epidemics, plagues, famines, wars, and earthquakes have all worked out the eternal purpose and glorified the Most High. From the first human prayer to the last mortal sigh, from the first note of finite praise to the everlasting hallelujah, *"all things work together for good to those who love God, to those who are the called according to His purpose"* (Rom. 8:28). All things are *"of Him and through Him and to Him."*

His Matchless Grace

This great principle is seen most clearly in the grand work of divine grace. Here everything is of God and through God and to God. The great plan of salvation was not drawn by human hands. It is no concoction of priests or no elaborate scheme of clergymen. Grace first moved the heart of God and joined with divine sovereignty to ordain a plan of salvation. This plan was the offspring of a wisdom no less than divine. No one but God could have imagined a way of salvation such as that which the Gospel presents—a way so just to God, so safe to man. The thought of divine substitution and the sacrifice of God on man's behalf could never have suggested itself to the most educated of all God's creatures. God Himself suggested it, and the plan is *"of Him."*

His Perfect Plan

Since the great plan is *"of Him,"* so are the details. God ordained the time when the first promise would be proclaimed, who would receive that promise, and who would deliver it. He ordained the hour when the great Promise-keeper would come, when Jesus Christ would appear, of whom He would be born, by whom He would be betrayed, what death He would die, when He would rise, and in what manner He would ascend.

Need I say more? He knew who would accept the Mediator, to whom the Gospel would be preached, and who would be the favored individuals who would respond to the gift of salvation. He settled in His own mind the name of every one of His chosen and the time when each elect vessel would be put upon the wheel to be fashioned according to His will. He determined what pangs of conviction would be felt when the time of faith came and how much of holy light and enjoyment would be bestowed. All this was purposed ahead of time. He settled how long the chosen vessel would be glazing in the fire and when it would be taken up, made perfect by heavenly workmanship, to adorn the palace of God Most High. From the Lord's wisdom, every stitch in the noble tapestry of salvation most surely comes.

The Incomparable Redeemer

Nor must we stop here. *"Through Him,"* all these things come. Through His Spirit, the promise came at last, for He inspired the prophets and holy men of old. *"Through Him,"* the Son of God was born of the Virgin Mary by the power of the Holy Spirit. *"Through Him,"* sustained by that Spirit, the Son of God lived His thirty-three years of perfection. In the great redemption, God alone is exalted. Jesus sweat in Gethsemane and bled on Calvary.

None stood with our Savior there. He trod that winepress alone (Isa. 63:3). His own arm brought salvation, and His own arm upheld Him (v. 5). Redemption was through God alone.

Not one soul was ever redeemed by human suffering. No spirit was freed by self-reproach, but all *"through Him."* And as *"through Him"* the Atonement came, so *"through Him"* the application of the Atonement comes. By the power of the Spirit, the Gospel is preached daily. Upheld by the Holy Spirit, pastors, teachers, and elders still remain with the church. The energy of the Spirit continues to go forth with the Word to the hearts of the chosen; still is *"Christ crucified"* (1 Cor. 1:23). God is in the Word, and through Him men are called, converted, and saved.

God Alone Should Be Praised

My beloved, beyond a doubt, we must confess that this great plan of salvation is all *"to Him."* We do not have a note of praise to spare for another. Silenced forever with everlasting confusion be those who would retain a single word of praise for man or angel in the work of grace. You fools! Who can be praised but God, for who but God determined to give His Son Jesus? You scoundrels! Will you rob Christ of His glory? Will you steal the jewels out of His crown when He so dearly bought them with drops of His precious blood?

You who love darkness rather than light, will you glorify man's will above the energy of the Holy Spirit? Will you worship your own freedom and dignity? God forgive you. As for His saints, they will always sing, "To God, to God alone be all the glory. From the first to the last, let Him who is the Alpha and the Omega have all the praise. Let His name be extolled, world without end."

When the great plan of grace is fully developed and you and I stand on the hilltops of glory, what a wondrous scene will open up before us! We will see more clearly then than now, how all things sprang from the fountainhead of God's love, how they all flowed through the channel of the Savior's mediation, and how they all worked together to the glory of the same God from whom they came. The great plan of grace, then, bears out this principle of our text.

Salvation Is of God

The word holds good, dear friends, in the case of every individual believer. Let this be a matter for personal inquiry. Why am I saved? Because of any goodness in me or any superiority in my constitution? Of whom comes my salvation? My spirit cannot hesitate a single moment. How could a new heart come out of the old one? Who can bring a clean thing out of what is unclean? Not one. How can the spirit come out of the flesh? *"That which is born of the flesh is flesh, and that which is born of the Spirit is spirit"* (John 3:6).

My soul, you must be quite clear about this: if there is any faith, hope, or spiritual life in you, it must have come from God. Can any Christian who possesses vital godliness argue with this statement? I am persuaded he cannot. If any man should claim any honor to his own physical makeup, I must, with all charity, doubt whether he knows anything at all about the matter.

Faith Comes from God

My soul, since your salvation must have come from God because He thought of it, planned it, and then gave it to you, did it not also come to you through God? It came through faith, but where did that faith have its origin? Was it not from the operation of the Holy Spirit? And what did you believe in? Did you believe in your own strength or in your own good resolution? No, you believed in Jesus, your Lord.

Did not the first ray of spiritual light you ever received come from God? Did you not look entirely away from yourself and to the Savior? The light that you now have, does it not always come to you in the same way: by being done once and for all with the creature, with the flesh, with human merit, and resting with childlike confidence upon the finished work and righteousness of the Lord Jesus Christ? Dear reader, is not your salvation, if you are indeed saved, entirely *"through"* God as well as *"of"* God?

Who is it that enables you to pray every day? Who keeps you from temptation? By what grace are you led onward in spiritual duty? Who upholds you when your foot would trip? Are you not conscious that there is a power other than your own? For my part, dear friends, I know that I am not being taken to heaven against my will. But my nature is still so desperate and so prone to evil that I feel myself floating against its current. It seems as if all we can do is to kick and rebel against sovereign grace, while sovereign grace says, "I will save you. I will have you, whatever you may do. I will overcome your raging corruption. I will revive you out of your lethargy and take you to heaven in a fiery chariot of afflictions, if not by any other means. I will drag you to paradise rather than let you be lost."

Is this not your experience? Have you not found that if the strong hand of God were taken from your soul, instead of going on to heaven, you would go back to eternal damnation? Is it not through God that you are saved? And, believer, is it not *"to Him"*? Will you take one single jewel out of His crown? Oh, there is not one of you who would wish to praise himself. There is no song we sing more sweetly than the song of grace. No hymn seems more in keeping with our own experience than this:

> Grace all the work will crown,
> Through everlasting days;
> It lays in heaven the topmost stone,
> And well deserves the praise.

Whoever will may glorify the dignity of humanity; whoever will may boast of the power of free will. We cannot do it. We have found our nature to be very depraved, and our wills to be under bondage. We must, even if other creatures do not, honor that changeless, omnipotent grace that has made us what we are. It will continue to keep us until it brings us to the right hand of God in everlasting glory.

The Harvest Is from God

In every work that the Christian is enabled to do, he should bear in mind the principle of the text. Some of you are privileged to work in the Sunday school, and you have had many conversions in your classes. Others have had success in distributing tracts, going from house to house to try to bring souls to Christ. Some of us, too, have the honor of being sent to preach the Gospel in every place, and we have had an abundant harvest of souls.

Some of us seem to have received the promised blessing to its fullest extent. The Lord has made our spiritual children like the sand of the sea (Isa. 48:19). Therefore, it is necessary for us to remember that *"of Him and through Him and to Him are all things."*

"Of Him." Who makes you unique? What do you have that you have not received? The burning heart, the tearful eye, the prayerful soul—all these qualifications for usefulness come *"of Him."* The eloquent mouth, the pleading tongue must have been educated and given by Him. The diverse gifts of the Spirit by which the church is edified all proceed from Him. Who is Paul? Who is Apollos or Cephas? Who are all these but the messengers of God (1 Cor. 3:4–5), in whom the Spirit works, *"distributing to each one individually as He wills"* (1 Cor. 12:11)?

When the preacher has achieved his usefulness, he knows that all his success comes through God. If a man thinks himself capable of stirring up a revival, of encouraging even one saint or leading one sinner to repentance, he is a fool. We might as well attempt to move the stars, shake the world, or grasp a lightning flash in the palm of our hand as think we can save a soul or even stir saints out of their lethargy.

Spiritual work must be done by the Spirit. Every good thing comes from God (James 1:17). The preacher may be strong like Samson when God is with him; he will be like Samson in his degradation and shame when God is not with him. Beloved, no man was ever brought to God except through God, or ever will be. Our nation will never again be stirred up into the celestial heat of piety except by the presence of the Holy Spirit anew. I strongly desire that we would have more of the abiding sense of the Spirit's work among us, that we would look more to Him, rest less in machinery and men, and trust more in that divine but invisible Agent who works all good things in the hearts of men.

Beloved, it is through God that every good thing comes, and I am sure it is *"to Him."* We cannot take credit for a single convert. We are thankful for growing churches, but we give the glory alone to Him. Give glory to humans, and they become boastful. Honor yourselves as a church, and God will soon dishonor you. Let us lay every gift upon His altar, bring every lamb of the fold to the feet of the Good Shepherd. When we go out to fish for souls, let us realize that we only fill the net because He taught us how to throw it on the right side; when we take them, they are His, not ours.

What poor little things we are, and yet we think we do so much. The pen might say, "I wrote Milton's *Paradise Lost*." Ah, poor pen! You could not have dotted an "i" or crossed a "t" if Milton's hand had not moved you. The preacher could not have done anything if God had not helped him. The ax might cry, "I have felled forests. I have made the cedar bow its head and laid the stalwart oak in the dust." No, you did not, for if it had not been for the arm that wielded you, even a shrub would have been too much for you to cut down. Will the sword say, "I won the victory. I shed the blood of the mighty. I caused the shield to be cast away?" No, it was the warrior, who with his courage and might made you of service in battle, but apart from this, you are less than nothing. In all that God does through us, let us continue to give Him the praise. Then He will continue to be with us in our efforts; otherwise, He will take His smile from us, and we will be left as weak men.

PRACTICAL APPLICATION OF THE DOCTRINE

Perhaps I have tried your patience in my efforts to clearly present this simple but very useful principle. But before I move to the topic of devotion, I would like to make a practical application of the truth of this doctrine. Beloved, if it is true that all things are *"through Him and to Him,"* do you not think that those doctrines are most likely to be correct and most worthy to be held that are most in keeping with this truth?

The Doctrine of Election

There are certain Christian doctrines commonly called Calvinistic, which I think commend themselves to the minds of all thoughtful persons for this reason mainly: they ascribe to God everything.

Consider the doctrine of election. Why is a man saved? Is it the result of his own will or God's will? Did he choose God, or did God choose him? The answer "man chose God" is clearly untrue because it glorifies man. God's answer is this: *"You did not choose Me, but I chose you"* (John 15:16). God *"chose us in Him before the foundation of the world...having predestined us to adoption as sons by Jesus Christ to Himself"* (Eph. 1:4–5). His will is the hinge of the whole matter and turns the balance. Ascribing the power of choice to God, I feel that I am in keeping with the doctrine of our text.

The Doctrine of Calling

Then take effectual calling. By what power is a man called? Some say that it is by the energy of man's own will or that while God gives man grace, it depends upon him to make use of it. Some do not make use of the grace and they perish. Others make use of the grace and are saved, saved by their own willingness to allow grace to be effective.

I, on the other hand, say that a man is not saved against his will, but he is made willing by the operation of the Holy Spirit. A mighty grace draws the man, disarms him, makes a new creature of him, and he is saved. I believe that the calling that saves the soul is a calling that owes nothing at all to man, but comes from God. The creature does not initiate the calling, but God molds the man like a potter molds clay. Clearly, the calling, I think, must be through God, for it coincides with the principle, *"Of Him and through Him and to Him are all things."*

The Power of the Blood

Next comes the question of particular redemption. Some insist that men are redeemed not because Christ died, but because their choice to accept salvation gives power to the blood of Christ. They say that believing is necessary in order to make the blood of Christ effective for redemption. I believe the very opposite. Namely, that the blood of Christ has in itself the power to redeem, and that it does redeem, and that faith does not give efficacy to the blood. Faith is only the proof that the blood has redeemed a man. Therefore, I believe that Christ redeemed all who will ultimately attain eternal life. I do not believe that He redeemed the damned. I think that the doctrine that men by their wills give power to the blood of Christ is derogatory to the Lord Jesus; instead, I believe that He laid down His life for His sheep, and that His laying down His life for the sheep involved and secured the salvation of every one of them. I believe this because I hold that *"of Him and through Him and to Him are all things."*

Man's Utter Corruption

Consider the total depravity of the race and its original corruption, a doctrine that is hated by those who lift up poor human nature; nevertheless, this doctrine is true. We believe that man must be entirely lost and ruined because if there is some good thing in him, then it cannot be said that *"of Him and through Him and to Him are all things."* If there are some traces of virtue and some remnants of power left in the race of man, then some things are of man, and to man will some things be. But if all things are of God, then in man there must be nothing. Man must be regarded as ruined—hopelessly ruined— bruised and mangled by the Fall, and his salvation must be described as being, from the first to the last, in every jot and tittle, a result of that almighty grace of God. The grace of God chose him, at length redeemed him, ultimately called him, constantly preserved him, and perfectly will present him before the Father's throne.

I put these doctrines before you from the teachings of that mighty servant of God, John Calvin. I honor him not as the formulator of these doctrines, but as one through whom God spoke, and one who, next to the apostle Paul, presented truth more clearly than any other man who ever breathed. He knew more of Scripture, and explained it more clearly than any other. Luther may have had as much courage, but when he saw one truth, like a bull, he shut his eyes and dashed against the enemy, breaking down gates, bolts, and bars to clear a way for the Word. But Calvin, following in the opened pathway—with a clear eye, searching Scripture, ever acknowledging that of God and through God and to God are all things—mapped out the whole plan with a delightful clearness, which could have come only from the Spirit of God. That man of God set forth the doctrines in so excellent and admirable a manner that we cannot too much bless the Lord who sent him, or too much pray that others like him may be honest and sincere in the work of the Lord.

This much is sufficient regarding doctrine. Now let us look briefly at devotion.

DEVOTION

The apostle puts his pen back into the ink bottle and falls on his knees. He cannot help it—he must have a doxology. *"To whom be glory forever. Amen."* Beloved, let us imitate this devotion. I think that this sentence should be the prayer, the motto, for every one of us.

Our Solitary Goal

"To whom be glory forever." This should be the single desire of the Christian. I take it that he should not have twenty wishes, but only one. He may desire to see his family well brought up, but only so that God may be glorified forever. He may wish for prosperity in his business, but only so far as it may help him to promote this praise: *"To whom be glory forever."* He may desire to attain more gifts and more graces, but his only purpose should be that God would be glorified forever. This one thing I know, Christian. You are not acting as you should when you are moved by any other motive than the one motive of your Lord's glory. As a Christian, you are "of God and through God"; I pray for you to be "to God." Let nothing ever set your heart beating but love for Him. Let this ambition fire your soul. May this be the foundation of every enterprise into which you enter and your sustaining motive whenever your zeal would grow chilly. Make God your only object. Depend upon it. Where self begins, sorrow begins. But if God is my supreme delight and only object:

> To me 'tis equal whether love ordain
> My life or death—appoint me ease or pain.

To me there will be no choice, when my eye singly looks to God's glory, whether I will be torn in pieces by wild beasts or live in comfort, whether I will be full of despondency or full of hope. If God is glorified in my mortal body, my soul will rest content.

Our Constant Desire

When I wake up in the morning, may my soul greet God with gratitude.

> Wake, and lift up thyself, my heart,
> And with the angels bear thy part,
> Who all night long unwearied sing
> High praises to the eternal King.

While at work, let me be looking for ways in which I can glorify Him. If I am walking in the fields, let my desire be that the trees will clap their hands in His praise. May the sun in its motion shine out the Master's glory. May the stars reflect His praise. It is yours, dear ones, to use your tongues to make the silent beauties of creation praise their God. Never be silent when there are opportunities, and you will never be silent for lack of opportunities. At night, fall asleep still praising your God. As you close your eyes, let your last thought be, "How sweet to rest upon the Savior's heart!"

In afflictions, praise Him. Out of the fires, let your song rise. On your sickbed, extol Him. Dying, let Him have your sweetest notes. In combat with death, the last great enemy, let your shouts of victory be all for Him. When you have broken the bondage of mortality and come into the freedom of immortal spirits, then, in a nobler, sweeter song, you will sing His praise. Let this be your constant thought: *"To Him be glory and dominion forever and ever. Amen"* (Rev. 1:6).

Our Earnest Thought

Do not speak of God's glory with cold words or think of it with a chilly heart; instead, feel, "I must praise Him. If I cannot praise Him where I am, I will break through these tight chains and get where I can." Sometimes you will wish that you were bodiless so that you could praise Him as the immortal spirits do. I must praise Him. Bought by His precious blood, called by His Spirit, I cannot hold my tongue. My soul, can you be silent and dead? I must praise Him. Stand back, flesh. Away, you devils. Away, you troubles. I must sing, for if I refuse to sing, surely the very stones will speak (Luke 19:40).

Our Ever Increasing Praise

I hope, dear friends, that in your earnestness, your praise will also be growing. Let there be an expanding desire to praise Him of whom and through whom are all things. You blessed Him in your youth. Do not be content with the praises you gave Him then. Has God prospered you in business? Give Him more as He has given you more. Has God given you experience? Then praise Him by better faith than you exercised at first. Does your knowledge grow? Then you can sing more sweetly. Are you happier than you once were? Have you been restored from sickness, and has your sorrow been turned into peace and joy? Then give Him more music. Put more spices in your censer, more fragrant frankincense, sweeter sugar. Oh, I long to serve Him every day, lifting up my heart from Sabbath to Sabbath until I reach the never-ending Sabbath. Reaching from sanctification to sanctification, from love to love, from strength to strength, I will appear before my God!

In closing, let me urge you to make this desire practical. If you really glorify God, take care to do it not with lip service, which dies away in the wind, but with true reverence throughout your daily lives. Praise Him by your patience in pain, by your perseverance in duty, by your generosity to His cause, by your boldness in testimony, by your consecration to His work. Praise Him, my dear friends, not only in what you give to Him by your offerings, but praise Him every day by your service, according to the manner in which He has been pleased to bless you.

I wish I could have written more effectively, but the Holy Spirit can work better through our weaknesses. If you will try to teach these truths to yourselves, my friends, you will do it vastly better than I can. If you will meditate upon this text, *"Of Him and through Him and to Him are all things,"* I am sure you will be led to fall on your knees with the apostle, and say, *"To whom be glory forever."* Then you will rise up, and practically in your life, give Him honor, putting the *"Amen"* on this doxology by your own individual service to your great and gracious Lord. May He bless you now and accept your thank offering through Christ Jesus.

Chapter 5

Wonders

And praise the name of the LORD your God,
who has dealt wondrously with you.
—Joel 2:26

In the case mentioned in the second chapter of Joel, the nation of Israel had seriously gone astray. Therefore, they were visited by a very remarkable punishment. An unusual plague of locusts devoured all the fruit of the field, and the people were distressed by a severe famine. *"For the day of the LORD is great and very terrible; who can endure it?"* (Joel 2:11).

The prophet Joel was commissioned to urge the people of God to repent. If they listened to his earnest pleas, their future would be bright with mercy. Because of God's gracious hand upon them, they were moved to repent. They wept and cried to God. Then the same God who with His left hand had been amazing in discipline was with His right hand equally astonishing in blessing and enriching them. He loaded their floors with wheat, caused their vats to overflow with wine and oil, and repaid them for the years in which the locust had consumed their crops, so that they had plenty to eat and were satisfied. They praised the name of the Lord, who had *"dealt wondrously"* with them. (See Joel 2:24–26.) He treated them with wonders when He afflicted them and with wonders when He returned to them in mercy.

THE ISRAELITES SAW GOD'S WONDERS

It was no unusual thing for the nation of Israel to encounter wonders. They were cradled in extraordinary events. They grew up among miracles. They lived with surprises. The history of the favored tribes is a long list of miracles. Remember how the Lord brought them *"out of Egypt with a mighty hand and with an outstretched arm"* (Deut. 26:8)? What *"marvelous things He did in the sight of their fathers, in the land of Egypt, in the field of Zoan"* (Ps. 78:12). By wonders, they were led out of Egypt and brought through the sea, upon whose shore they sang triumphantly, *"Who is like You, O LORD, among the gods? Who is like You, glorious in holiness, fearful in praises, doing wonders?"* (Exod. 15:11).

Their course in the great howling wilderness for forty years was a march of wonders. When the manna dropped from heaven and the water leaped from the rock, the Lord *"dealt wondrously"* with them. Not a single day of the forty years opened or closed without wonders. The day was shaded by the cloudy pillar, and the night glowed with the light of the fiery pillar (Exod. 13:21). Not even when the desert journey was over did God's wonders cease. The river was divided before them: *"What ails you, O sea, that you fled? O Jordan, that you turned back?"* (Ps. 114:5).

They entered their land and began its conquest by a wonder, for the walls of Jericho fell flat to the ground. They continued its conquest by the same marvelous power, for mighty kings fled before them. The sun and moon stood still while they struck down hostile armies. When they had driven out the Canaanites and were established in the land of promise, they sinned greatly. But what wonders of deliverance God worked for them when they cried to Him in their trouble! Just remember the names of Gideon, Barak, Jephthah, and Samson, and you will see before you wonder after wonder. The Lord *"dealt wondrously"* with them.

GOD WORKS MIRACLES TODAY

In all these experiences, the Israelites were a type of true believers, for with all His chosen ones the Lord has *"dealt wondrously."* We frequently hear the complaint that we live in a boring age. We have no adventures now, and remarkable events are few. We are happy that it is so, for it has been well said: "Blessed are the times which have no history." If peace and prosperity are commonplace, long may the commonplace continue.

But no thoughtful man's life is uninteresting or devoid of marvels. A sincere life cannot be empty of memorable occurrences. He who thinks so must either be unspiritual or oblivious to his own inner history. He must be like the tribes of Israel in the wilderness of whom it is written, they *"forgot His works and His wonders that He had shown them"* (Ps. 78:11).

Foolish people run to fiction for wonders, but godly people can tell far greater wonders. The wonders of which we can speak far surpass the inventions of imagination. Truthfully, no dreamer could dream after such a fashion.

Our days and nights have far exceeded in marvel the tales found in the *Arabian Nights.* God *"does great things past finding out, yes, wonders without number"* (Job 9:10). I have seen a volume entitled *The World of Wonders* and another named *Ten Thousand Wonderful Things.* The believer is himself a world of wonders, and his life reveals ten thousand wonderful things. Mysteries, riddles, paradoxes, and miracles make up Christian experience.

Of these wonders I will try to write, according to that precept of David—*"Talk of all His wondrous works!"* (Ps. 105:2). I will examine them in the following manner: first, I will testify that God's dealings toward us have been full of wonder, leading us to praise Him as Jehovah our God; second, I will remark that because of this, we ought to look for wonders in the future, and if I may speak so paradoxically, it should not be surprising to us to see wonders; third, I will close by observing that in a future state, we will yet more clearly see that Jehovah has *"dealt wondrously"* with us.

PRAISE GOD FOR HIS MATCHLESS LOVE

God's Personal Love

The Lord's dealings with us up until now have been full of wonder, leading us to praise Him. Let us speak of what we know, what we have tasted, and what we have handled. The Lord has *"dealt wondrously"* toward us.

Begin at the beginning. It was no small wonder that He should love us before the earth ever was. Many other things could have involved Jehovah's thoughts besides thinking about man: *"What is man that You are mindful of him?"* (Ps. 8:4). And if He had to think of man, there were many kinds of thoughts that the Lord might have had toward man besides thoughts of love. Yet the Lord was mindful of us. Even though we are poor and needy, the Lord thinks about us. *"How precious also are Your thoughts to me, O God! How great is the sum of them!"* (Ps. 139:17).

Why were they thoughts of love? Gratitude and admiration toward God give us the only reply. It is a wonder of wonders that they should be thoughts of love for me! Each Christian will feel this to be the question in his own heart: "Why did divine love settle itself upon me?" Well might we say of our God what David said of Jonathan, *"Your love to me was wonderful"* (2 Sam. 1:26).

The song of the Virgin may be on our lips: *"He has put down the mighty from their thrones, and exalted the lowly"* (Luke 1:52). He has thought of us who were insignificant while the great ones of the earth have been passed by. Eternal love in its sovereignty is a marvel and *"comes from the LORD of hosts, who is wonderful in counsel and excellent in guidance"* (Isa. 28:29).

God's Faithful Love

That divine love should have continued faithfully, notwithstanding our unworthiness of it and the irritations with which we have tried it, is another wonder. The unchangeableness of His counsel calls for adoring wonder. Has there been a day since we have been responsible for our actions in which we have not tested the faithfulness of God by our transgressions? For forty years, the children of Israel provoked God in the wilderness. Sadly, were they not the prototypes of ourselves? Yet never, never has the Lord paused or changed in His love. As it is said of our blessed Redeemer, *"He loved them to the end"* (John 13:1). It is also true that the Father loves you. Rest in His love.

God's Covenantal Love

If divine love is in itself a wonder, friends, it is equally a wonder that because of this love, God should enter into covenant with us. He has promised us a thousand mercies and has engaged Himself to the performance of those promises in a remarkable way; this increases the comfort of the promise. He has given us His oath: *"I have made a covenant with My chosen, I have sworn to My servant David"* (Ps. 89:3). God has entered into covenant with us in the person of the Son of David, a covenant ordered in all things and sure, confirmed by oath and sealed by blood, by which He has bound Himself by His own word and oath, that in blessing, He will bless us and glorify His Son in us.

Behold and wonder—the Infinite enters into covenant with the finite; the Holy engages Himself to sinners. We, too, may sit before the Lord as David did, engulfed in astonishment, and then say from our heart of hearts, *"Who am I, O LORD God? And what is my house, that You have brought me this far?"* (1 Chron. 17:16).

It is equally wonderful that a part of the covenant states: *"I will be a Father to you, and you shall be My sons and daughters, says the LORD Almighty"* (2 Cor. 6:18). If God had wanted sons and daughters, besides the Only Begotten, He might have chosen the bright angels who outshine the sun. Why look here upon this anthill to choose an offspring out of such ants as we? Why did He come down in the person of His Son to make a match with our frail humanity? Oh, matchless grace, that God should adopt for His children those who were *"children of wrath"* (Eph. 2:3). Jesus looked at stones and said, *"God is able to raise up children to Abraham from these stones"* (Matt. 3:9). Beloved, *"behold what manner of love the Father has bestowed on us, that we should be called children of God"* (1 John 3:1).

God's Secure Love

As His sons and daughters, let us admire and wonder that the Lord should stake His honor upon bringing us securely to heaven. For in the covenant, He has pledged all His attributes for His people's security. He cannot be a glorious God unless His people ultimately are a glorified people. He cannot be true unless His people are kept to the end, for He has pledged His honor for their safety.

Jesus has said, *"I give them eternal life, and they shall never perish; neither shall anyone snatch them out of My hand"* (John 10:28). Yes, the Lord Himself has declared that *"Israel shall be saved by the LORD with an everlasting salvation; you shall not be ashamed or disgraced forever and ever"* (Isa. 45:17), and that *"Heaven and earth will pass away, but My words will by no means pass away"* (Matt. 24:35). The sun and moon will cease their shining, but He will not *"alter the word that has gone out of* [His] *lips"* (Ps. 89:34). Will He not do what He has said? Will He not make good what He has spoken?

God's Incarnational Love

By shifting the kaleidoscope, we will get another view of the same matchless wonders. The Lord has acted wondrously for us. Having loved us and covenanted with us, He gave us His only begotten Son to be born in our nature and, in that nature, to suffer even unto death! I will not attempt to show to you that this is a wonder. I believe that the angels, though they have known of the Incarnation nearly two thousand years, have never ceased from astonishment for one single moment.

That God, the Word, should become flesh and live among us and that He should bleed and die exceeds everything that is wonderful. That Jesus Christ, the King of Kings, should be a Servant of servants, that He who wrapped the earth in the ocean like swaddling clothes and spread on the firmament its garments of blue should wrap Himself with a towel and wash His disciples' feet is, beyond measure, a wonder! Yet He is virtually fulfilling this sacred office every day in His perpetual intercession for His people and in all His acts of love toward them. This is indeed dealing wonderfully with us.

In the gift of the Lord Jesus, we have obtained pardon, justification, sanctification, and eternal life, all of which contain a mine of wonders. Perhaps to repentant hearts, the chief of all these is the forgiveness of sin, and of such sins as ours—

> Great God of wonders! all Thy ways
>   Are matchless, God-like, and divine;
> But the fair glories of Thy grace
>   More God-like and unrivaled shine:
> Who is a pardoning God like Thee?
> Or who has grace so rich and free?
>
> In wonder lost, with trembling joy
>   We take the pardon of our God;
> Pardon for crimes of deepest dye,
>   A pardon bought with Jesus' blood:
> Who is a pardoning God like Thee?
> Or who has grace so rich and free?

God's Abundant Love

Having given us His Son, the Lord has also, in Him, *"given to us all things that pertain to life and godliness"* (2 Pet. 1:3). I put these things into words and sum them up, but, indeed, there is an ocean of thought in every syllable I write, for the Lord has given us this world and worlds to come. He has given us earth and heaven. He has given us time and eternity: *"All are yours. And you are Christ's, and Christ is God's"* (1 Cor. 3:22–23). Believer, there is nothing in divine care that is not yours, for *"all things work together for good to those who love God, to those who are the called according to His purpose"* (Rom. 8:28).

That which looks harmful is good to you, and the good has a goodness in it that you do not yet perceive, an inner core of excellent mercy that will be opened for you in due time through the abounding wisdom of God. Walk now like Abraham of old. Lift up your eyes to the north and to the south, to the east and to the west, for all this has God given to you in giving you His Son. He has *"dealt wondrously"* with us in this respect.

He has made the angels to be our servants, glad to wait upon us and to bear us up in their hands for fear that we might dash our feet against a stone (Ps. 91:12). Making the angels to be our servants, He has made the angels' home to be our home, only He has brightened it with a special glory for us. It is not written that many mansions are prepared especially for angels, but Jesus our Lord has gone *"to prepare a place"* for us (John 14:2), made ready especially for our delight. He has not given us merely the angels of heaven, heaven itself, and Jesus to prepare a place for us, but He has given us Himself to be our God, for *"'the LORD is my portion,' says my soul"* (Lam. 3:24). He has confirmed it: *"I will be their God, and they shall be My people"* (Ezek. 37:27). He has *"dealt wondrously"* for us then.

Beloved, I now ask you to consider your own experiences. You who know the Lord, remember that the Lord has worked miracles within us. Not so long ago, we were dead. He made us live. We were loathsome lepers, and He made us whole. We were blind, and He gave us sight. We were lame, and He made us leap. We were prisoners, and He set us free. We were condemned, and He justified us by His grace.

The changes that He made in us were incredible. We were astounded as we experienced them. We marveled to feel the hardness of our hearts removed. Years ago, nothing could move us; neither fear nor love could stir us, but the Lord came and struck us as Moses hit the rock. Immediately, the waters of penitence gushed out. Why, the rock itself became a standing pool.

What a change the grace of God makes in the matter of repentance. The very man who was hard as a diamond one day becomes like putty the next. He who never cared for God, nor wept for sin, hates himself with the deepest and humblest remorse. Then, blessed be God, another wonderful change comes over him. The man whom you saw broken in heart for sin, unable to derive a grain of comfort from anything around him, all of a sudden believes on the name of Jesus as it is brought home with power to his soul by the Holy Spirit. Right away, he wipes his eyes as his mourning is turned to dancing. He becomes supremely happy through faith and breaks forth with such songs as this:

> I will praise Thee every day,
> Now Thine anger is turned away.
> Comfortable thoughts arise,
> From the bleeding sacrifice.

At times, has your soul been as hard and cold as marble, and yet suddenly, has it dissolved as ice melts in the sun? Has your soul been tossed up and down like the Atlantic in a rage, and yet suddenly, has it been made smooth as a mirror by God's wondrous hand? Your experience within you, I am sure, is a verification of the statement that Jehovah your God *"has dealt wondrously with you."*

God's Amazing Love

What tremendous conflicts our souls have known! What wonderful victories we have won through divine grace! Immortal sins, as they seemed to be, have received their deadly wound. Unconquerable lusts have been defeated. Our victories will never be forgotten, but the crown of them will be put on the head of Him who enables us to be more than conquerors. And what wonderful revelations God has granted to us. Has He not often poured a flood of light upon a truth we saw but dimly before and made our spirits leap for joy? He has opened our eyes to behold wondrous things out of His law (Ps. 119:18). Why, I bear witness that sometimes when my Lord Jesus Christ Himself has been revealed in my soul, I have been unable to collect my thoughts of joy, much less to put them into a language that would make them intelligible to other people. For the glory and the beauty are transcendent, and the love and the fellowship of Christ are transporting, ecstatic, ravishing. They bear the soul away.

God's Consoling Love

These wonders of revelation bring with them wonders of consolation. Have we not seen dying Christians full of life? Have we not seen them sinking in body, but soaring in soul? Sick, weak, feeble, and breathless, yet full of glory, they are ready to burst with the new wine of the kingdom, which has been poured into their frail vessels. Have we not heard some of them sing between their groans such songs as only God's sweet love could have taught them? The angels could sing no sweeter songs, and assuredly, they know no sweeter themes! Yes, beloved, our inner experience has been full of wonders. We have committed terrible sins and suffered tremendous sorrows, but we have received wonderful pardons and enjoyed wonderful raptures. We have passed through challenging fights, but we have gained amazing victories; wondrous has been our darkness, but we have seen marvelous light.

Coleridge has said that "in wonder all philosophy begins, in wonder it ends, and wonder fills the interspace." Truly, I can say the same of all vital godliness. Another has said that "the wise man wonders once in his life, but that is always." The same may be affirmed of the man made wise unto salvation. It may be true that our first wonder is born of ignorance. At any rate, much of ignorance mingles with its surprise, but certainly, afterwards, our wonder becomes the parent of adoration. We wonder when we grow in grace, not because we are not familiar with it, but we wonder at what we do know of amazing love and grace. Our children look up at the stars and think they are like little pinholes in the sky. They say,

> Twinkle, twinkle, little star,
> How I wonder what you are.

But when the astronomer looks through his telescope and gazes at those celestial bodies, he says with greater truth,

> How I wonder what you are!

Man's wonder grows with his knowledge. As he wades into the river of wisdom, he is less and less able to keep the foothold of calm reason and is more and more likely to be uplifted and carried off his feet by the current. It is so with Christian experience: the more we know of God, the more wonderful His dealings to us appear.

God's Victorious Love

Now, beloved, I must ask you once again to consider that, as the Lord has *"dealt wondrously"* toward us, wondrously for us, and wondrously in us, so he has also *"dealt wondrously"* by us. What a field of battle, what a throne of victory the poor child of God often becomes! Why, in this narrow plot of human clay, the powers of heaven and hell have mustered all their armies many times for conflict, and God and His grace and truth have fought with Satan in our hearts. Bless God that on that battlefield, God has won many victories over the allied armies of the world, the flesh, and the Devil.

We have been garrisoned against besieging sins, delivered by the force of heavenly arms from the power of our corruption and brought forth by sovereign grace to delight in the Lord our God. When we get to heaven, we will be *"a wondrous sign"* (Zech. 3:8), established as signs and wonders forever, immortal witnesses of God's boundless grace. In the celestial streets, we will announce His deeds of infinite love:

> *To the intent that now the manifold wisdom of God might be made known by the church to the principalities and powers in the heavenly*

places, according to the eternal purpose which
He accomplished in Christ Jesus our Lord.

(Eph. 3:10–11)

Will not the angels say to one another, "Here are men and women who were tempted in a thousand ways, who carried about with them bodies of sin and death, who were tried with all sorts of afflictions and passed through much tribulation—but see what they are now! See how God has triumphed in them. See how He has defeated the Evil One and overcome the powers of evil. For these tempted ones have come through great tribulation and have washed their robes and made them white in the blood of the Lamb (Rev. 7:14). There is not one in whom God has been defeated. Not one in whom the eternal purpose has failed. Not one in whom electing love has been baffled. Not one in whom the power of Christ's blood has been ineffective. Not one to whom the Spirit came without winning a complete victory. Let us praise God anew and sing *'Worthy is the Lamb'* (Rev. 5:12)."

Our God has also worked miraculously through some of us, fulfilling His promise: *"The people who know their God shall be strong, and carry out great exploits"* (Dan. 11:32). His *"strength is made perfect in weakness"* (2 Cor. 12:9). There are some among us whose lips have led many in worship, and yet they confess themselves to be emptiness itself. Their word has brought life to the dead, yet in themselves they have no power. They have scattered the King's enemies although they are by nature weak as water. God's ministers are but *"trumpets of rams' horns"*

(Josh. 6:4), yet when God has blown through them, the blast has made the walls of Jericho rock, reel, and fall to the ground. They are but lamps enclosed in earthen pitchers, and yet by them, Midian has been routed. (See Judges 7.) Glory be to the name of Jehovah our God for this.

Thus you see God has done wondrously by us. Praise Him; praise Him! Will you pause and sing a psalm of praise now? People, praise Him! You who know His wonders, praise Him! *"Let the redeemed of the LORD say so, whom He has redeemed from the hand of the enemy"* (Ps. 107:2). Let them sacrifice the sacrifices of thanksgiving, and bless the name of the Lord. *"Praise the name of the LORD your God, who has dealt wondrously with you."*

> Let the redeemed of the Lord
> The wonders of His grace record;
> How great His works! How kind His ways!
> Let every tongue pronounce His praise.

LOOK FOR GOD'S WONDERS

Our second and practical point is this: we ought to expect wonders. Are you struggling under a horrible sense of your sinfulness? Do you seem to yourself to be the blackest of all unpardoned souls, the nearest to being damned already of all living beings? Do you think that it would be the greatest wonder that ever occurred since the world began if you were to be saved? I have the most precious thought to tell you (may the Holy Spirit place it in your heart): the Lord is a God of wonders. He does only wondrous things.

Are You Spiritually Cold?

He delights to find in our sin and misery, room, scope, and opportunity for wonders of grace. Cast yourself upon the mercy of our matchless God, and He will make you as much a wonder of grace as you have been a wonder of sin. Possibly some are saying, "I do not feel my sin as I should. I wish I did. I feel numb and insensible. If I feel anything, it is only a sort of regret that I do not have any feeling."

My dear friend, you will be a wonder, too, if God revives you and makes you tender of heart. In you, too, He finds scope for grace. He wakes the dead. He kills and makes alive. He wounds and He heals. Cry to the Lord to make you sensitive through His wounding and killing work. If your heart is cold as ice, ask Him to melt it, for it is written, *"He sends out His word and melts them"* (Ps. 147:18). Is it not promised in His own covenant, *"I will put a new spirit within them, and take the stony heart out of their flesh, and give them a heart of flesh"* (Ezek. 11:19)? The Lord of love delights to work these transformations.

Are You Sad?

Do you feel depressed in spirit? Have you felt that way a long time? Are you one of those who feel sad without the light of the sun? Would it not be a great marvel if you should become one of the happiest of God's people? It would. I believe you will be, for God delights to work wonders. He can bring His servants out of the darkest prison. He enabled Paul and Silas to sing in the inner dungeon, and then He brought them out. He can make you sing now and bring you out into clear, full liberty. He can do it today: *"The LORD gives freedom to the prisoners. The LORD opens the eyes of the blind; the LORD raises those who are bowed down"* (Ps. 146:7). The prisoners of the Lord will not be prisoners forever. Release from jail is coming, and they will leap for joy.

Are You Sick?

Are you lying at death's door? Do you cry like the singer Heman, *"My soul is full of troubles, and my life draws near to the grave"* (Ps. 88:3)? Perhaps you are sick in body, distracted in mind. Do you feel you are ready to die, and therefore you think that it is all over with you? What a desperate state you seem to be in. It would be a wonderful thing if you would obtain light and comfort, would it not?

Again, let me remind you that if it would be wonderful, it is all the more probable with the Lord. He is very compassionate. He delights in being merciful. The Lord heals the brokenhearted and binds up their wounds. Wonderful are His ways of consoling the mournful. Great is His wisdom and discernment in devising ways to bring back His banished ones. Therefore, *"ascribe greatness to our God"* (Deut. 32:3). Look to Him for mercy. Believe in God for immeasurable, tender affection.

Do You Need a Savior?

If I presented a little christ for little sinners, some of you would be wise to read elsewhere. But since I have a divine calling to proclaim a great Savior for great sinners, One who is able to help us through great difficulties and to overcome great sins, why, He is the very Savior for you. Bless Him, love Him, and trust Him, and He will work wonders in your spirit.

Have You Fallen Away?

Possibly I write to someone who has desperately backslidden. It has been years since you knew the truth, and you have, by your sins, fastened chains of iron on your soul. Well, the Lord whom you have grieved is full of compassion and can take those chains off. Yes, He can break the gates of brass and cut bars of iron in half. The Lord can work wonders of deliverance for His imprisoned children.

Are Your Problems Ordinary?

"Oh," cries another, "my case is merely a commonplace one. There is nothing remarkable about me." My dear friend, would it not be a wonderful thing if God were to save such an ordinary, insignificant person as you? Well, rest in Him, trust in Him, and there will be wonderful works performed for you also. You will be one of those amazing people in whom God's grace is fully revealed.

Do You Feel Hopeless?

If there is anything about you, beloved, that seems to make your salvation difficult or even impossible, if there is anything in your case that causes you to feel hopeless and desperate, whether it is in your secular or your spiritual life, I would recommend that you take your case to the God of wonders.

See whether He does not before long make you say, *"The LORD...has dealt wondrously with me."* To sinners who believe in Jesus, salvation is promised, and they will have it. To saints who trust in the Lord, deliverance is promised, and delivered they will be. God will work ten thousand wonders, but He will never allow His promises to fall to the ground.

Are You Expecting God to Answer?

I would earnestly remind all God's servants that we ought to expect wonderful answers to prayer. We should pray as if we expected the God of wonders to hear us. In times of trouble, we ought to expect to see wonderful deliverances. If we are confined by our circumstances, we should expect Him to provide a way of escape. Since we need a miracle, we should look to God to make it happen. We have grounds for expecting wonderful comfort if we are about to endure great troubles. We should look for wonderful joys between here and heaven. We ought to be on our watchtower, looking for wonderful discoveries of Christ's beauty and God's love. In fact, we should always be looking for wonders and should wonder if wonders do not happen.

In the church, we are permitted to expect wonders. We are too much in the habit of merely going to worship services and sitting down and hearing sermons; if half a dozen are converted, we are astonished. But we ought to expect thousands to be converted. If the church ever has faith enough to expect great things, she will see great things. When the church falls upon dark times and error mars her beauty, we may expect God to work wonders to purify and exalt her.

Our Wonderful God, Savior, and Holy Spirit

In the darkest medieval times, God found His witnesses. When the light threatened to die out, then Martin Luther came, a man raised up by God. A train of glorious men followed him. Never tremble; never despair; never be afraid. *"The LORD of hosts is with us; the God of Jacob is our refuge"* (Ps. 46:7). We worship the God of wonders who does only wonderful things.

Our Savior is also called *"Wonderful"* (Isa. 9:6). Stephen said of Him, *"Jesus of Nazareth, a Man attested by God to you by miracles, wonders, and signs"* (Acts 2:22).

Likewise, the Holy Spirit works wonders. He came at first with a *"rushing mighty wind"* and *"divided tongues"* and miraculous gifts (Acts 2:2–3). Even now, His wonders have not ceased. They have only become spiritual, instead of physical. But the Spirit of God is working mightily now.

I bear personal witness that God has worked wonders for us far beyond all human ability. We could not perform these wonders. We did not deserve these wonders. These are wonders that we could not have expected, could not have imagined, could not have comprehended. I may add, these are wonders for which, throughout eternity, we will never be able to praise God sufficiently though we spend our whole existence in adoring our wonder-working God! *"How great are His signs, and how mighty His wonders! His kingdom is an everlasting kingdom, and His dominion is from generation to generation"* (Dan. 4:3).

In Heaven, Our Wonder Will Increase

My last remark is this: in our future state, these wonders will be even clearer to us. If we were to read our Bibles attentively, we would be astonished to find how much there is about heaven in them. It is not true that we have mere glimpses, for if studiously investigated, the Word of God tells us wondrous things concerning the world to come.

Beloved, in the better land, we will wonder more than we do here, for there we will understand far more than we do now. We will have clearer views and wider perspectives. Our present capacities are narrow. There is scarcely room within our minds for great things, but in that bright world, the veil will be removed. *"For now we see in a mirror, dimly, but then face to face. Now* [we] *know in part, but then* [we] *shall know just as* [we] *also* [are] *known"* (1 Cor. 13:12).

In the heavenly mansions, our growing knowledge will excite in us increasing wonder. There we will sing the praise of Him who has *"dealt wondrously"* with us. I believe the poet was right when he said:

> And sing with wonder and surprise
> Thy loving-kindness in the skies.

We Will Know What We Missed

In our homes of endless bliss, we will see what we escaped. We will look down from our place at Abraham's side and see the sinner far off in torment.

(See Luke 16:22–23.) It will be a dreadful sight, but with hearts of gratitude, we will bless redeeming love, knowing that were it not for divine grace, that desperate fate would have been ours.

We Will Realize the Awfulness of Sin

In the heaven of perfect holiness, we will know the true character of sin. When we see the brightness of God's glory and the splendor of His holiness, sin will appear in all its hideousness. We will adore the matchless mercy that pardoned us. We will bless the precious blood that cleansed us though we had been defiled with such pollution. We think we praise God for forgiving our iniquities, and no doubt we do in some measure, but compared with the blessing that saints in heaven give to God for deliverance from sin, our praise is nothing. We do not know sin as they know it. We do not understand its blackness as they perceive it.

We Will Understand Life's Mysteries

Up in heaven, we will see our lives and God's dealings with us as a whole. A great many matters that now appear mysterious and complex, concerning which we can only walk by faith because our reason is baffled, will be so clear to us as to excite our joyous songs in heaven. "Now I see why I was laid aside when I wanted to be busy in God's work. Now I see why that dear child, whom I had hoped would be spared as a comfort to me during my old age, was taken away. Now I understand why my business was allowed to fail. Now I comprehend why that person was allowed to defame me. Now I see why I was attacked by inward fears and was permitted to struggle with them." Such will be our confessions when the day dawns and the shadows flee away. Then we will say and sing: "Our God has dealt wonderfully with us." We will feel that the best was done for us that even Eternal Wisdom could devise, and we will bless the name of the Lord.

We Will Rejoice in His Majesty

Reflect a moment, dear friends, and see further reasons for everlasting amazement. In heaven, we will see what God has lifted us up to be. We talk of being children of God. Do we fully understand what that means? We speak of heaven being ours. Do we know what we mean by that language? Truly *"it has not yet been revealed what we shall be, but we know that when He is revealed, we shall be like Him"* (1 John 3:2). Neither have our eyes seen nor our ears heard the *"things which God has prepared for those who love Him"* (1 Cor. 2:9).

When we stand on the sea of glass and hear the harpists, we will join their endless music. When we see Him who laid down His life for us, yes, see Him as He is, when we behold the Lamb of God, who by bowing to death lifted us up from our deadly fall, who by stripping Himself of His royalty, robed us with splendors, we will be amazed, astounded, and overwhelmed with wonder.

We Will See God

Above all, when we see God Himself, what will be our wonder! Within our minds, we will be able to behold the infinite Jehovah and hear His voice. When we come to speak with God familiarly and stand before that throne whose brightness today would blind us, when we know Him who fills all in all, we will be plunged into adoring wonder forever. I will not say we will be amazed to think He loved us. There is no need to say that. I will not say we will be filled with astonishment to think He ever saved us. Rather, how amazing it is that He should permit us to be His sons and daughters and should, at such enormous expense, bring us to dwell with Himself forever, making us partakers of His own nature, one with His own Son. We will *"praise the name of the* LORD *[our] God, who has dealt wondrously with* [us]*."*

Let the Praise Begin

I beg you to begin the music here. I long to spend my time perpetually adoring the God of wonders. I desire that we should rise above the spirit of discontent, the spirit that finds fault, mourns, moans, and laments, making complaints by which to provoke the Lord our God. Let it not be said of us, "They soon forgot His wonders" (Ps. 78:10–11). Let us go on singing to Him who does only wondrous things, speaking to one another of all His wondrous works. Day by day, hour by hour, let us admire our God, world without end.

Chapter 6

Inexcusable Irreverence and Ingratitude

*They are without excuse,
because, although they knew God,
they did not glorify Him as God,
nor were thankful.*
—Romans 1:20–21

This first chapter of the epistle to the Romans is such a terrifying portion of the Word of God that I hesitate to read it through aloud, even to myself. Read it and be startled at the terrible sins of the Gentile world. Unmentionable crimes were the common pleasures of those wicked ages, but this chapter is also a striking picture of heathenism today.

After a missionary had gone to a certain part of India and had given away New Testaments, a Hindu waited for him and asked this question: "Did you write that first chapter in the epistle to the Romans after you came here?" "No," replied the missionary. "I did not write it at all; it has been there nearly two

133

thousand years." The Hindu said, "Well, if it has not been written since you came here, all I can say is that it might have been written about us, for it is a fearfully true description of the sin of India."

It is also true of our cities—more accurate than some of us would like to admit. Even where I live, vices are committed, the very mention of which would make a modest person blush. However, I am not going to write about Hindus; they are far away. I am not going to write about ancient Romans; they lived a couple of thousand years ago. I am going to write about us and about people whom my text aptly fits. I fear that I am addressing some who are *"without excuse, because, although they knew God, they did not glorify Him as God, nor were thankful."*

LACK OF REVERENCE

The first charge against those who are mentioned in my text is lack of reverence. *"They knew God,"* but *"they did not glorify Him as God."* They knew that there was a God; they never denied His existence, but they had no reverence for His name. They did not give Him the respect to which He is entitled. They did not honor Him as God.

Never Thinking of God

That is still true of people today. Some never think of God. They go from year to year without any practical thought of Him. Not only is He not in their words, but also He is not in their thoughts. As the psalmist wrote, *"The wicked in his proud countenance*

does not seek God; God is in none of his thoughts"
(Ps. 10:4). Whether there is a God or not makes no
practical difference to the wicked. They have so little
esteem for Him that perhaps if we could prove that
there were no God, their consciences would feel re-
lieved.

There must be something very wrong with a
person who would prefer that there were no God.
"Well," says one, "I do not care much whether there
is a God or not; I am an agnostic." A gentleman once
told me that he was an agnostic. I replied, "That is a
Greek word, is it not? And the equivalent Latin word
is 'ignoramus.'" Somehow, he did not like it in Latin
nearly as much as in Greek. Oh, dear friends, I could
not bear to be an "ignoramus" or an "agnostic"
about God. I must have God; I cannot do without
Him. To me, He is as necessary as food to my body
and air to my lungs.

The sad thing is that many who believe that
there is a God do not glorify Him as God. They do
not even give Him a thought. I appeal to you to consider if this description applies to your life. Do you
go from the beginning of the week to the end without reflecting upon God at all? Could you do as well
without God as with Him? Must there not be something very terrible in the condition of your heart if,
as a creature, you can do without a thought of your
Creator—when He who has nourished you and
brought you up is nothing to you, one of whom you
never think?

Having a False Concept of God

Further, some have a misconception of God. The
true concept of God is that He is all in all. If God is

anything, we ought to make Him everything. You cannot put God in second place. He is almighty, all-wise, all-gracious, all-knowing, omnipresent. His power flows to every part of the universe. God is infinitely glorious, and unless we treat Him as such, we have not treated Him as He ought to be treated. If a king is assigned to open doors or do menial work, he is not honored as a king should be. Will the great God be made a servant to our desires? Will we put God aside, saying to Him: "When it is more convenient, I will send for You. When I have more money, I will make time for religion. When I can be religious and not lose anything by it, then I will seek You"? Do you treat God so? Oh, beware. This is high treason against the King of Kings! Wrong ideas of God, groveling thoughts of God, come under the censure of our text, *"Although they knew God, they did not glorify Him as God."*

Never Worshipping God

Again, dear friends, there are some who think of God a little, but they never offer Him any humble, spiritual worship. Do not imagine that God can be worshipped by anything that is merely mechanical or external, which is not from the heart. That god who is pleased with what some men call worship must be very strange indeed. I have been in churches and seen decorations that would have been a disgrace to a barroom, and I have said, "Is God pleased with this kind of thing?" Then I have been in fancier buildings where I have seen crucifixes and altars adorned in jewels befitting a bride. God cares not for jewels. Is your concept of God that He desires your gold, silver, brass, fine linen, and all these adornments? Do you think that He is like humans in this way?

Surely, you have a poor concept of God. When the organ peals out its melodious tones, but the organist's heart is not in the playing, do you think that God has ears like those of a man, ears that can be tickled with sweet sounds? Why have you brought Him down to your level? He is spiritual; the music that delights Him is the love of a true heart, the prayer of a seeking spirit. He has better music than all your organs and drums can ever bring to Him. If He wanted music, He would not need to ask you to produce it. Winds and waves make melodies transcendently superior to all that your most notable musicians can compose.

Does He want candles when His touch turns mountains to great altars, smoking with the incense of praise to the God of creation? Oh, beloved, I fear that it has been true of many who externally appeared to be devout that *"although they knew God, they did not glorify Him as God."* Weep over your sin: now you have glorified Him as God. Fall on your face and be nothing before the Most High: now you have glorified Him as God. Accept His righteousness; adore His bleeding Son; trust in His infinite compassion. Now you have glorified him as God, for *"God is Spirit, and those who worship Him must worship in spirit and truth"* (John 4:24). How far, my dear readers, have you complied with that command?

Not Serving God

Further, the people mentioned in our text did not glorify God, for they did not obediently serve

Him. My friends, have you served God? Have you looked upon yourselves as servants of God? When you awoke in the morning, did you say, "What does God expect me to do today?" When you have reviewed the day, have you applied this test: "How far have I endeavored to serve God today?" Many are the servants of themselves, and no master is more tyrannical than unsanctified self. Many are toiling like slaves for wealth, for honor, for respectability, for possessions. But remember, if the Lord is God and He made us, we are bound to serve Him. How is it that God has kept you alive all these years, and yet you have never glorified Him as God by serving Him at all? This is a very solemn question. I would like everyone whom it concerns to examine his own conscience.

Not Trusting God

There is another charge to be brought against those who knew God but did not glorify Him: they did not trust Him. The place for man is under the shadow of God's wings. Since He made me, I ought to seek Him in the hour of trouble. In the time of my need, I should turn to His resources. If I feel unhappy, I should look to Him for comfort. Beloved, are there some of you who have never trusted God? You run to your neighbors as soon as you are in difficulty. You trust your old uncle, but you never trust your heavenly Father. What a wretched business is this if God, who is all truth and all love, does not have the confidence of His own creatures! Remember how the Lord spoke through Jeremiah:

> *Cursed is the man who trusts in man and
> makes flesh his strength, whose heart departs
> from the LORD. For he shall be like a shrub in
> the desert, and shall not see when good comes,
> but shall inhabit the parched places in the
> wilderness, in a salt land which is not inhab-
> ited. Blessed is the man who trusts in the
> LORD, and whose hope is the LORD. For he
> shall be like a tree planted by the waters,
> which spreads out its roots by the river, and
> will not fear when heat comes; but its leaf will
> be green, and will not be anxious in the year of
> drought, nor will cease from yielding fruit.*
>
> (Jer. 17:5–8)

The people mentioned in the text knew God, but
they did not trust Him.

Not Talking with God

In addition to this, they did not seek to com-
mune with Him. Are there not some of you who have
never tried to speak to God? It never occurred to
you, did it? And God has not spoken to you; at least,
you have not known whose voice it was when He did
speak. It is a very sad business when a child, who
has been at home with his father and mother for
years, has never spoken to them. He has come down
in the morning and eaten his breakfast; he has come
in and devoured his lunch; he has eaten his dinner
with them night after night, but he has never spoken to them. Would you have a boy of that kind living with you? You would be obliged to say, "John,
you must go; it hurts me to send you away, but I
cannot bear to have you sitting here in silence. When

139

I speak to you, you never answer me." Some of you cannot remember a time when you spoke to God or God spoke to you; it is so very long ago, if it ever did occur.

Speaking Irreverently

Equally tragic is the man who calls upon God with a foul and blasphemous oath. When he tells a lie, he calls upon God to witness it. Yes, he has broken the silence, but it would have been better not to have spoken than to have uttered those vile blasphemies against the Most High. His horrible words have *"reached the ears of the Lord of Sabaoth"* (James 5:4). As the Lord lives, that man will have to answer to the great Judge of all men. His words will have condemned him unless he seeks God's face and finds forgiveness through His Son. Our Savior said that for every idle word that men speak, they will have to give an account in the Day of Judgment (Matt. 12:36). How much more will they be required to answer for every evil, false, slanderous, or blasphemous word they have spoken!

Many persons have never uttered an oath. Even though they are scrupulously careful about speaking the truth, they have never talked with God. They are wretched creatures indeed. Although they may be wealthy and prosperous, they have missed the highest good, the best blessing that man can know.

Not Seeking Reconciliation

Some, although they know God, do not glorify Him. They are aware of their separation from God, but they do not want to be reconciled to Him. Perfect reconciliation between God and men is possible. All who believe in Christ Jesus are at once forgiven; they are adopted into the family of God; they drink of the love of God; they are saved with an everlasting salvation. But knowing these truths in their minds never stirs up any desire for them in their hearts. Whether they are reconciled or unreconciled does not trouble them. In plain language, they are saying, "I defy God; I neither want His love, nor fear His hate; I lift my face before His thunderbolts and dare Him to do His worst." Oh, fatal defiance of the blessed God! May the Spirit of God work upon your conscience now to make you see the evil of this condition and turn from it!

I feel deeply troubled to have to write these words, but I am speaking of what many consciences would confess to be true. You live, some of you, knowing God, but not glorifying Him as God.

LACK OF GRATITUDE

Now I take from our text the second accusation, which is certainly quite as sad as the first. Those who are mentioned by Paul are accused of ingratitude. It is said of them that *although they knew God, they did not glorify Him as God, nor were thankful.*

I cannot say anything much worse of a person than that he is not thankful to those who have been his benefactors. When you say that someone is not thankful to God, you have said about the worst thing you can say. Do not look merely at the people who lived in Paul's day, but at those who are living now.

You will soon see how many people are guilty of ingratitude. In God's High Court of Justice, they stand accused of many counts in the indictment that is brought against them.

Ignoring God's Moral Laws

First, God's law is despised. Intelligent young men and women, if they are wise, say, "We wish that we knew what we should do in order to live long and be happy. We would like to know what to avoid so that we don't hurt ourselves." Well, the Ten Commandments provide clear instruction for moral living. They tell what will damage us and what will benefit us. We ought to be very thankful to have such plain directions. God says, "You shall" and "You shall not."

Although God has taken the trouble to give us this map of the way and to direct us on the only right road, some have despised the heavenly guide. They have gone directly against that law; in fact, it looks as if the very existence of the law has been a provocation to them to break it. Is not this an example of dreadful ingratitude?

Whenever God says, "You shall not," it is because it would be harmful to us to do it. Likewise, when ice on ponds is not strong enough to hold a person's weight, signs that say "Dangerous" are put up. Who but a fool would go where that danger signal is? The Ten Commandments indicate what is dangerous: even more, what is fatal. They help us to know how to keep clear of all that is forbidden. They are given in love to protect us from evil.

Dishonoring the Sabbath

Next, God's day is dishonored by those who are not thankful to Him. In His great mercy, God has given us one day in seven in which to rest and to think of holy things. Of the seven days God gave to us in a week, He said to take six, and use them for our business (Exod. 20:9). Yet we think that we must have the seventh as well. It is like someone who, while traveling, comes upon a poor man in distress. Having but seven shillings, the generous person gives the poor man six, but when the wretch scrambles to his feet, he follows his benefactor to knock him down and steal the seventh shilling from him.

How many people do this! The Sabbath is their day for sports, for amusement, for anything but the service and worship of God. They rob God of His day, though it is but one in seven. This is base ungratefulness. Could you confess that you have been guilty of it? If so, let no more Sabbaths be wasted. Let those sacred hours—and all the week between— be spent in diligent searching after God. Then, when you have found Him, the Lord's Day will be the brightest gem of all the seven, and you will sing with hymnwriter Isaac Watts:

> Welcome, sweet day of rest,
> That saw the Lord arise;
> Welcome to this reviving breast,
> And these rejoicing eyes!

Neglecting the Bible

Moreover, God's Book is neglected by these ungrateful beings. Was there ever such a Book so full of wisdom, so full of love? Look at it on bended knee and find heaven between its pages. Although God has given us this wonderful Book, many do not take the trouble to read it. What ingratitude! It is a Father's love letter to His child, but the child leaves it unread! Here is a Book unlike any other. God has exercised His omniscience to make it a perfect Book for all ranks and conditions of men in all periods of the world's history, yet such is man's ingratitude that he turns away from it.

Refusing God's Son

However, there is something much worse: God's Son is rejected by the unthankful. God has only one Son, and such a Son: one with Himself, infinite, holy, His delight! From the heart of God, He was sent to this earth. Taking our nature, the Son became a servant, dying the death of a criminal, the death of the cross, all to save us. He died for the guilty, for men who were His enemies.

Thinking about my own guilt that caused His death, I could burst into tears. This must be one of the mysteries that angels cannot comprehend: after Christ has suffered and died for us, some sinners choose not to be saved by Him. They refuse to be washed in the fountain filled with blood; they reject eternal life, even though it streamed from the five great wounds of His body. They choose hell rather than salvation by His blood. They are so in love with their dire enemy, sin, that they will not be reconciled to God even by the death of His Son.

Oh, ingratitude, you have reached your utmost limit now, for you have *"trampled the Son of God underfoot, counted the blood of the covenant by which* [you were] *sanctified a common thing, and insulted the Spirit of grace"* (Heb. 10:29). Is this not terrible?

Forgetting His Protection

I could stop here. But for the sake of pricking the consciences of some, I want to say, dear friends, that some people are so ungrateful that they forget God's deliverances. Some years ago, I spoke with a cavalryman who had miraculously survived a disastrous, bloody battle. Almost all the saddles emptied; shots and shells flew to the right and left; death mowed down the whole brigade; yet he escaped. When he told me so, I took him by the hand; I could not help it, though he was a stranger to me. With tears in my eyes, I said, "Sir, I hope that you are God's man after such a deliverance as that." Regretfully, he still had not given his heart to Christ.

I know of a man who has been in several shipwrecks, but if he does not pay attention to God, he will be shipwrecked for all eternity! Another has had yellow fever. Oh, there are worse fevers than that for those who will not respond to God.

I cannot cite all the cases of miraculous deliverance, but I do not doubt that some of you have been between the jaws of death. You have looked over the edge of that dread precipice beneath which is the fathomless abyss. You vowed that if God would spare your life, you would never be what you were before; in truth, you are not, for you are worse than ever. You are sinning now against light and in shameful ingratitude. May God have mercy on you!

Ignoring God's Blessings

How often, dear friends, is there ingratitude on the part of unconverted men in acknowledging God's divine care? Why, look at some of you! You have never missed a meal in your lives. When you went to the table, there was always something on it. You never had to lose a night's rest for lack of a bed. From your childhood, you have had all that your hearts could wish. If God has treated you so, while many are crushed with poverty, should He not have some gratitude from you?

You had a good mother; you had a tender father; you have gone from one relationship to another with increasing comfort. You are spared; your parents are spared; your spouse and children are spared. Indeed, God has made your path very smooth. Some of you are succeeding in business while others are failing; some of you have loving support at home while others have been widowed, or their children have died one after the other. Will you never be grateful? Hard, hard heart, will you never break? Will His compassion not persuade you? Must there be a storm of wrath to break you in pieces, like a potter's vessel? Will not love and tenderness melt you? I appeal to those whose paths have been so full of mercies: think of God and turn to Him with sincere repentance and faith.

Yet one says, "I have had good luck." What can be worse than that? Here is a prime example of ingratitude to God: calling His good gifts "good luck." Some respond, "Well, you know, I have been a very hardworking man." I know you have, but who gave you the strength to work? Others say, "I have had a good supply of brains while others have not." Did you make your own brains? Do you not feel that any man who talks about his own superior intelligence writes *FOOL* across his forehead in capital letters? We owe everything to God; will we give God nothing? Will we have no gratitude for Him from whom all blessings come? God forgive us if it has been so, and give us grace to change our ways at once!

Resisting God's Spirit

Another example of ingratitude of which many are guilty is resisting God's Spirit. The Spirit of God comes to them and gently touches them. Perhaps He has come to you, and you have said, "Do not talk quite so plainly to me. Give me a little comfort, a little breathing space; do not be quite so hard on me." He has come to you a good many times, and you have tried to drive your Best Friend from your heart. You have been so stingy with Him that when He came to lead you to Christ, you summoned all your strength to resist Him. The Devil came to help you, and, up until now, you have opposed the Spirit of God with some degree of success. The Lord have mercy on you! But how true is our text, even of many who attend church: *"Although they knew God, they did not glorify Him as God, nor were thankful."*

LACK OF UNDERSTANDING

I will conclude with my third point, which is, that this lack of reverence and gratitude occurred in spite of their knowledge. *"Although they knew God, they did not glorify Him as God, nor were thankful."*

Will you kindly notice that according to the text, knowledge is of no use if it does not lead to holy practice? *"They knew God."* It was no good to them to know God, for *"they did not glorify Him as God."* So, my theological friends who know so much that you can split hairs over doctrines, it does not matter what you think or what you know, unless it leads you to glorify God and to be thankful. In fact, your knowledge may be a millstone around your neck that will plunge you to eternal misery unless your knowledge is turned to holy practice.

Knowledge Brings Responsibility

Indeed, knowledge will increase the responsibility of those who are irreverent and ungrateful. Paul said, *"Although they knew God, they did not glorify Him as God, nor were thankful."* Whatever excuse might be made for those who have never heard of God, there was none for these people.

My dear readers, you also are *"without excuse."* Many of you have had godly parents, you have attended a gospel ministry, your Sunday school teachers and Christian friends have taught you the way of salvation; you are not ignorant. If you do not glorify God, if you are not thankful to Him, *"it will be more tolerable for the land of Sodom and Gomorrah in the day of judgment"* (Matt. 10:15) than for you, for they never had the privileges that you have scorned.

Remember how the Savior reproached the cities where most of His mighty works were done because they did not repent. They did not honor Him as God even though He had shown Himself to them time and time again. Instead of hearing His words of approval, they were rebuked:

> *Woe to you, Chorazin! Woe to you, Bethsaida!*
> *For if the mighty works which were done in*
> *you had been done in Tyre and Sidon, they*
> *would have repented long ago in sackcloth and*
> *ashes.* (Matt. 11:21)

It is a great wonder that the people who saw Christ's mighty works did not repent.

Repentance Brings Eternal Life

I wish, dear friends, that you could get out of this state of not glorifying God and not being thankful. Surely, as the Spirit of God speaks to your consciences, you will want to say, "I cannot bear to be in such a dreadful condition with regard to God any longer." May God enable you to repent.

Change your mind. That is the meaning of the word *repent*. Change your mind and say, "I will glorify God. He is the meaning of life. There is a Creator. There must be an omnipotent, all-wise Being. I will worship Him. I will say in my heart that this God will be my God, and I will trust Him."

Then remember the years that are past. They involve a great debt, and you cannot pay it. If you go on serving God without a flaw until the end of your lives, there is still the old debt due. There are the years that are gone, and *"God requires an account of what is past"* (Eccl. 3:15). But hear what He has done for us. He has given His dear Son to bear *"our sins in His own body on the tree"* (1 Pet. 2:24). If you will trust in Christ, you can know for sure that you are forgiven. *"Look"*—that is His word—*"Look to Me, and be saved, all you ends of the earth"* (Isa. 45:22).

When the brass serpent was lifted up, all that those who were bitten had to do was to look at it; everyone who looked, lived. If any man of that crowd had looked at Moses, he would not have been healed. If he had looked at the fiery serpents and tried to pull them off, he would not have been healed. But when he looked to the brass serpent, and his eyes caught the gleam of the metal, the deadly serpents' bites were healed, and the man lived. (See Numbers 21:6–9.) Look to Jesus. Look now. May God, the Holy Spirit, lead you to do so!

"I do not feel able," says one. That is looking to yourself. "I do not feel my need enough," says another. That is trusting in your sense of need. Away with everything that is in you or about you. Just trust Christ, and you will immediately be saved. Whoever will simply look to Jesus will be saved on the spot. However great your iniquities, however stony your heart, however despairing your mind, look, look, look, look. Then, when you look to Christ, your ingratitude will be forgiven, and it will die. You will love Him who has loved you, and you will be saved, and saved forever.

Let Renewal Begin

I breathe an earnest prayer that our taking to heart these great truths might be the beginning of a revival. May it come today, and may all who do not know Christ be carried away by that blessed tide of mighty grace that will sweep them off their feet and land them safely on the Rock of Ages!

Will you, dear friend, pray for revival? At the family altar or at your bedside, will you make it a special subject of prayer that men who knew God, but glorified Him not as God and were not thankful, may now turn to God?

If I could reach some of you who are living without Christ, I would like to do what the Roman ambassadors used to do. When they came to a king who was at war with the empire, they said to him, "Will you have peace with Rome or not?" If he said that he must have time to think it over, the ambassador would draw a ring around the man, and say, "You must decide before you cross that line, for if you do not say 'Peace' before you step out of it, Rome will crush you with her armies." If I could, I would draw a ring around you. I would pray for the Lord to hold you fast and not let you go until you say, *"Lord, I believe; help my unbelief"* (Mark 9:24). May God bless you for Jesus' sake.

Chapter 7

The Singing Army

*So Judah gathered together
to ask help from the LORD.*
—2 Chronicles 20:4

Jerusalem was startled by sudden news. For a great while, quiet preparations had been made in the distant countries beyond Jordan. In the mountainous region of Edom, the enemies of Israel had been getting ready. Their workshops in the city of Petra had been ringing with the sound of hammers beating their pruning hooks into spears and swords.

They were now coming down in hordes. There were three great nations, assisted by the odds and ends of all the nations round about, so that a great company eager for plunder was drawn up in battle. They had heard about the riches of the temple at Jerusalem. They knew that the people of Judea had been flourishing for years, and now they were coming to kill, to destroy, to loot, and to steal. They were as numerous as grasshoppers or locusts. What were the people of God to do? How were these poor Judeans to defend themselves?

Their immediate resort was to their God. They do not appear to have gathered up their armor and swords with any particular anxiety. The case was so altogether hopeless as far as they were concerned that it was useless to look to anything beneath the skies. Since they were driven from all visible earthly assistance, they were compelled to lift up their eyes to God. Their godly king Jehoshaphat helped them to do so.

A general fast was proclaimed, and the preparation to meet the armies of Moab, Ammon, and Edom was prayer. No doubt if the Ammonites had heard of it, they would have laughed. Edom would have scoffed, and Moab would have cursed those who prayed.

"What! Do they suppose that their prayers can defeat us?" would have been the sneer of their adversaries. Yet this was Israel's artillery: this was their eighty-one ton gun. When it was ready, it would launch one missile, and only one, and that would crush three nations at once. God's people resorted only to the arm invisible, the arm omnipotent, and they did well and wisely.

Now, if the Lord will teach us to imitate them, and by His grace enable us while doing it, we will have learned a great lesson. This writer needs to learn it as much as anybody, and he prays that each one of you may be scholars in the school of faith, becoming proficient in the divine art of prayer and praise.

How They Asked for Help

First, they asked for help by calling for a general fast and prayer, but what was the style of that prayer in which they approached the Lord?

They Prayed Confidently

The answer is that they asked for help in a way that expressed their confidence:

> LORD *God of our fathers, are You not God in heaven, and do You not rule over all the kingdoms of the nations, and in Your hand is there not power and might, so that no one is able to withstand You?*   (2 Chron. 20:6)

If we begin by doubting, our prayer will falter. Faith is the tendon of Achilles, and if that is cut, it is not possible for us to wrestle with God. As long as we have that strong sinew, that mighty tendon unhurt, we can prevail with God in prayer. It is a rule of the kingdom, though God often goes beyond it, *"According to your faith let it be to you"* (Matt. 9:29).

I have known Him to give us a hundred times as much as our faith would expect, but, friends, I have never known Him to give less. That could not possibly be. I can safely say that this is His minimum rule: *"According to your faith let it be to you."* Therefore, when you are in a time of trouble, ask God for help, believing that He is able to give it. Ask expecting that He will give it.

Do not grieve the Spirit of God by unworthy doubts and mistrusts. These things will be like fiery arrows in your soul and will drink up the very life of your strength. However hard the struggle and difficult the trial, if you seek the Lord, seek Him in the confidence He deserves.

They Remembered God's Faithfulness

Then they sought God, appealing to His past acts. This is a type of prayer that has been very common among the saints, and it has proved to be very powerful:

> *Are You not our God, who drove out the inhabitants of this land before Your people Israel, and gave it to the descendants of Abraham Your friend forever?* (2 Chron. 20:7)

Remember what God has done for you, and then say, as a sweet refrain, *"Jesus Christ is the same yesterday, today, and forever"* (Heb. 13:8). When you are praying, recall what He was yesterday to you. If there are no present manifestations of divine favor, remember the past—the days of old—*"the years of the right hand of the Most High"* (Ps. 77:10). He has been gracious to you. Can you tell how gracious? He has abounded toward you in loving-kindness, tenderness, and faithfulness. He has faithfully *"led* [you] *through the wilderness, through a land of deserts and pits, through a land of drought"* (Jer. 2:6).

If in six troubles He has delivered you, will you not trust Him for seven? If you get to sixty troubles, can you trust Him for sixty-one? Some of you have been carried by God all your lives, and now, your hair has turned gray. How long do you expect to live? Do you think you have ten years left? Well, do you think that the Lord who has blessed you for seventy years will not keep you for the other ten?

We say that we ought always to trust a man until he deceives us. We consider a man to be honest, until we find him otherwise. Let it be so with God, I beg you. Since we have found Him good, faithful, true, kind, and tender, let us not think harshly of Him now that we have come into crisis.

Let us come to Him, and say, "Are You not our God? Did You not bring us up out of the horrible pit and out of the miry clay (Ps. 40:2)? Did You not bring us out of the Egypt of our sin? Surely You have not brought us into this wilderness to destroy us. (See Deut. 1:27.) Will You leave us now? True, we are unworthy, but we always were, and if You wanted a reason for leaving us, You had ten thousand reasons long ago." Say with the prophet, *"Do not be furious, O LORD, nor remember iniquity forever; indeed, please look; we all are Your people!"* (Isa. 64:9). That is the style of pleading that prevails. Imitate these men of old who asked for help by recalling the past.

They Relied on His Promises

Going a little further in their prayer, we see that the people of Judea pleaded the promise of God that was made at the time Solomon dedicated the temple:

> *If disaster comes upon us...we will stand before this temple and in Your presence (for Your name is in this temple), and cry out to You in our affliction, and You will hear and save.*
> (2 Chron. 20:9)

He who understands the promise of God and grasps God with the promise does and must prevail.

I have known of a man unable to grasp anything. Objects slip away from him because his hand
is slippery. Yet I have seen him take some sand in
his hand, and then he has been able to get a grip. I
like to plunge my hand into the promises, and then I
find myself able to grasp the mighty faithfulness of
God with a grip of determination.

An omnipotent plea with God is: *"Do as You
have said"* (2 Sam. 7:25). You know how a man nails
you when he brings your very words before you.
"There," he says, "that is what you said you would
do. You pledged to do this of your own free will." You
cannot get away from it. It is that way with the
saints if they swear to something. Even if it means
that they will be hurt by following through, they
must be true to their word.

Of the saints' Master, it is always true. *"Has He
said, and will He not do? Or has He spoken, and will
He not make it good?"* (Num. 23:19). Here is a
mighty instrument to be used in prayer: "Lord, You
have said it; now *'do as You have said.'* You have
said, *'Many are the afflictions of the righteous, but
the LORD delivers him out of them all'* (Ps. 34:19).
You have said, *'He shall deliver you in six troubles,
yes, in seven no evil shall touch you'* (Job 5:19). You
have said, *'Surely blessing I will bless you'* (Heb.
6:14). You have said, *'Be strong and of good courage;
do not be afraid, nor be dismayed, for the LORD your
God is with you wherever you go'* (Josh. 1:9). You
have said, *'Your sandals shall be iron and bronze; as
your days, so shall your strength be'* (Deut. 33:25).
Lord, here are Your promises for my need." With
such a plea, you must prevail with a faithful God.

They Admitted Their Weakness

Next, as these people asked for help, they confessed their own unhappy condition. There is great power in that. One of the strongest pleas for generosity is the urgency of poverty, and one of the most prevailing arguments to be used in prayer with God is a truthful statement of our condition—a confession of our sad state. So they said to the Lord:

> *O our God, will You not judge them? For we have no power against this great multitude that is coming against us; nor do we know what to do, but our eyes are upon You.*
>
> (2 Chron. 20:12)

They had no might; they had no plan. Sometimes even if you cannot do something, it is a little comfort to know how it might be done if you had the power. But these perplexed people could not do it, nor did they even know how to do it. They were bewildered. A little nation like Judah, surrounded by these powerful enemies, truly had no might. Their weakness and ignorance were great pleas. Their logic was divine: *"Nor do we know what to do, but our eyes are upon You."*

It was as if they had said, "If we could do it ourselves, you might tell us, 'Go and do it. What did I give you the strength for, but so that you could use it?' But because we have no strength, and we do not know what to do, we come and just present the case at Your feet and say, *'Our eyes are upon You.'*"

Perhaps you think that is not praying. I tell you, it is the most powerful form of prayer—just to set your case before God, just to lay bare all your sorrow and all your needs, and then say, "Lord, there it is."

In some of our cities, people are not permitted to beg in the streets. The police will not allow it, and I venture to say, that is a wise regulation. But what does the needy person do? Have you not seen him? He is dressed like a peasant and looks half starved. His knees can be seen through an old pair of corduroys as he stoops. He does not beg. He only sits down at the corner of the road. He knows quite well that the very sight of his condition is enough.

There are some people on the streets whose faces are a fortune to them; pale, thin, and woebegone, they appeal more eloquently than words. Their manner of shivering and their remarkably ill appearance, although they are not sick, take in people who are continually being duped. All the world knows that it is the look of the thing, the very appearance and show of sorrow, that prevails with people more than any words that are used.

Therefore, when you cannot pray in words, go and lay bare your sorrow before God. Show your soul. Tell God what it is that burdens and distresses you, and you will prevail with the bounteous heart of our God. He is not moved by eloquence of words or oratory of tongue, but is swift to answer the true oratory, the true eloquence of real distress, and is as able to detect false misery as to relieve real sorrow.

Do you recall any particular times of trial? I do. At any rate, there is one common affliction that has overwhelmed us all: the great affliction of sin. When sin, with its many offenses, becomes clear to us under conviction, and we do not know how to face one single sin or to answer one of a thousand of the charges that might be brought against us; when we feel that we have no strength whatsoever; when we realize that through sin we have brought ourselves into such terrible circumstances, and we do not know how to get out of them, though we feel that we must; when we turn to the right and that way seems blocked, and the left seems equally closed to us; when we dare not go back, and we cannot go forward, how wonderfully God clears the way! In a miraculous manner, we find our enemies dead that we thought were going to kill us! As for those who were going to rob us, we are enriched by them. Instead of plundering us, they fall, and their riches become our right. We take them home with us, rejoicing. Oh, what wonders God can do!

He loves for us to state the difficulty we are in. Then when He gets us out of it, we may remember the sorry condition that we were in. It was a real disaster and a time of genuine trial, yet the Lord redeemed us from it.

They Declared Their Trust

What did they do after asking for help, after pleading the promise and confessing their condition? Why, they expressed their confidence in God. They said, *"Our eyes are upon You"* (2 Chron. 20:12). What did they mean by that? They meant, "Lord, if help does come, it must come from You. We are looking to You for our rescue. It cannot come from anywhere else, so we look to You. But we believe it will come. Men will not look for what they know will not come. We feel sure it will come. We do not know how, so we are looking to You. We do not know when, but we are looking to you. We do not know what You would have us to do, but we are looking to You, Lord. Lord, we are looking."

It is a great attitude. Do you not know that is the way you are saved—by looking to Jesus? And that is the way you must be saved—all the way between here and heaven. Whatever trouble comes, looking will save you—looking, often waiting, looking like the weary watcher from the tower when he wants to see the gray tints of the coming morning, when the night is long and he is weary, but still looking. *"Our eyes are upon You."* They are full of tears, but still they are fixed on You. They are getting drowsy with sleep, but still they are focused on You. With the eyes that we have, we look to You.

I have sometimes thanked the Lord that He did not say, "See Jesus—see Me and be saved." What He has said is "Look." Sometimes if you cannot see, you have still done your part if you have looked—looked into the darkness. Lord, Your cross would give me such joy if I could see it. I cannot quite see it. It looms very indistinctly on my gaze, but I do look. It is looking, you know, that saves. For as we look, the eyes get stronger, and we are enlightened. And so in this case, they looked, and they found deliverance. May God help us, brothers and sisters, to do the same.

HOW THEY RECEIVED HELP

Their Fears Were Allayed

Their help came to them, first, by a message from God. They received a fresh assurance of God's goodness. Jahaziel, a new prophet, was raised up, and he spoke with new words: *"Do not be afraid nor dismayed because of this great multitude, for the battle is not yours, but God's"* (2 Chron. 20:15). Now, in our case, we will not have a new promise. That would not be possible:

> What more can He say
> Than to you He has said,
> To you who to Jesus
> For refuge have fled?

But you will have that promise sweetly brought home to your soul. The Spirit of God will bear witness with that promise, strengthening and comforting you. You will receive deliverance even before deliverance comes.

It often happens that to be rescued from the fear of trouble is the main need. To be quieted, calmed, and assured is really to be saved from the sting of trial. The trial itself is nothing if it does not bring a sting to your soul. If your heart is not troubled, then there is not much trouble in anything else. All the poverty and pain in the world would be powerless if the evil of it did not enter into the soul and distress it. So in this emergency, God began to answer His people by quieting them: *"Do not be afraid nor dismayed because of this great multitude, for the battle is not yours, but God's."*

As that gracious promise calmed their fears, they were able to face the impending attack. Then they received distinct direction as to what to do on the next day, which was to be the day of the assault. That direction was *"Tomorrow go down against them"* (2 Chron. 20:16).

How often God has given His people deliverance by quieting them before He directs them to act. Already the steps they have taken in looking to Him have delivered them before they knew it. As we will see, the Israelites, by marching out with songs and praises to meet their foes, were doing the best possible thing to rout them. As I have already said, there is no doubt that their enemies were unable to comprehend such a defense as this. They must have supposed that there was some treachery or ambush intended, so they began to slay each other. Israel had nothing to do but to keep on singing.

Then came the real providence: they received actual deliverance. When the people of Judah came to their foes, they found there were no foes. There they lay all rigid and dead. None of the men of might could raise their hands against those whom God had favored.

After this fashion, God will deliver you, beloved. In answer to your prayers, He will be your defense. Therefore, sing unto His name. Did He not deliver you in this way when you went out to meet the great army of your sins? You saw that Christ had put them away, and your heart danced within you as you said, *"There is therefore now no condemnation to those who are in Christ Jesus"* (Rom. 8:1). He has slain our sins, and they can curse us no more.

So it has been with a great many troubles that have appeared to you to be overwhelming. When you have come to them, they have disappeared. They have been cleared out of your way as you have advanced, and you have had nothing to do but sing and praise the name of the Lord.

They Responded by Worshipping

Finally, and this is the main point, let us note how they acted after they had prayed and heard God's voice. They asked for help and received it. How did they then behave?

Well, first, as soon as they had an assurance that God would deliver them, they worshipped. That is one of the purposes of trials—to revive in us the spirit of devotion and communion with God. And when mercy comes on the back of great trouble, it leads us sweetly to prayer. I maintain that there never was such profound worship in all of Jerusalem as there was that day. After Jahaziel, that young son of the Levites, had stood and delivered the Word of the Lord, the king and all the people bowed their heads and honored the God of Israel. You could have heard the sound of the wind rustling the trees at the time, for they were so hushed and quiet. Oh, when you know that the Lord means to deliver you, bow your head and give Him the quiet, deep, solemn worship of your spirit.

I do not suppose that many people practice the Quakers' form of worship, though an occasional experience of it would do us a world of good. To sit still before the Lord and to adore, and to adore, and to adore again and again, and still again, braces the spirit and clears the soul for the understanding of eternal realities.

They worshipped, but why did they do it? They were not delivered. No. But they were sure they were going to be delivered. Their enemies were not dead. No. They were all alive, but they were sure they would be dead, so they had a time of worship, and their devotion rose from trustful and grateful hearts. May we get into a worshipping frame of mind and be kept in it. Then God will appear for our help.

They Proceeded to Praise

As soon as the worship time had ended, or rather just before it had quite finished, they began to praise. Up went the loud voices of the trained singers under the leadership of the chief musician, and they praised the name of the Lord. They sang, as we do:

> For His mercies will endure,
> Ever faithful, ever sure.

That is the way you should deal with God. Before deliverance comes, praise Him. Praise Him for what is coming; adore Him for what He is going to do. No song is so sweet, I think, in the ear of God as the song of a man who blesses Him for grace he has not tasted yet—for what he has not received, but what he is sure will come. The praise of gratitude for the past is sweet, but that praise is sweeter that adores God for the future in full confidence that all will be well. Therefore, take down your harps from the willows (Ps. 137:2). Oh, you people, praise the name of the Lord.

Though the fig tree may not blossom, nor fruit be on the vines; though the labor of the olive may fail, and the fields yield no food; though the flock may be cut off from the fold, and there be no herd in the stalls; yet I will rejoice

in the LORD, I will joy in the God of my salva-
tion.   (Hab. 3:17–18)

Though there is not enough income to meet
your needs, and you are almost at necessity's door,
still bless the Lord, whose mighty providence cannot
fail, and will not fail, as long as there is one of His
children to be provided for. Your song while you are
still in distress will be sweet music to the ear of God.

They Practiced Obedience

After they had worshipped and sung, the next
thing these people did was to act. They went forth
marching. If there were unbelievers in Jerusalem, I
know what they said. They stood at the gates and
said, "Well, this is foolishness. These Moabites and
Ammonites have come to kill you. They will do it,
but you might as well wait until they get to you. You
are just going to deliver yourselves to them." That
would be the idea of unbelief, and that is also how it
sometimes seems to our little faith when we go and
commit ourselves to God. "What! Are you going on
your knees to confess your guilt before God and admit that you deserve to be lost? Are you going to
withdraw every excuse and apology, every trust of
your own, and give yourself up, as it were, to de-
struction?" Yes, that is exactly the thing to do, and it
is the highest wisdom to do it. We are going out of
the city marching away according to orders, and if
we are to give ourselves up, so we will.

Perhaps, in your case, you are planning to do
something about which everybody else says, "Now,
that will be very foolish. You should be crafty. You

should show a little cunning." "No," you reply, "I cannot do other than I am directed. I must do the right thing." Probably that will turn out to be the very best thing in the world to have done. The shortest distance between any two points is by a straight line. The straight way will always be better than the crooked way. In the long run, it is always so. Go right out in the name of God. Meet your difficulties calmly and fairly. Do not have any plans or tricks, but just commit yourself to God. That is the way by which you may confidently expect to find deliverance. These people of old went out of the city.

They Started to Sing

Notice again, that as they went out, they went out singing. They sang before they left the city and as they left the city. When the adversary came in sight, they began to sing again. The trumpet sounded, the harps rang out their notes, and the musicians shouted for joy. This was the song:

> For His mercies will endure,
> Ever faithful, ever sure.

It must have had a great significance when they sang:

> *To Him who struck down great kings, for His mercy endures forever; and slew famous kings, for His mercy endures forever; Sihon king of the Amorites, for His mercy endures forever; and Og king of Bashan, for His mercy endures forever.* (Ps. 136:17–20)

Why, every singer as he sang those lines, which look to us like mere repetition, must have felt how applicable they were to their present condition when there was a Moabite and an Edomite and an Ammonite to be overthrown in the name of the mighty God whose mercy endures forever. So they kept on singing. You will observe that while they were singing, God was accomplishing the great deliverance for them.

They Reaped the Reward of Their Trust

When the singing stopped, they prepared to gather up the spoil. What a different activity from what they had expected! You can see them stripping the bodies; taking off the helmets of gold and the armor of brass, the jewels from the ears and from around the necks of the princes; robbing the dead of their Babylonian garments and their wedges of gold; heaping up the tents—the rich tents of the Eastern nations—until they said to each other, "We do not know what to do."

But the difficulty was different from what might have happened to them at first. Previously, they did not know what to do because of their weakness in the presence of their foes, but now the difficulty was because of the greatness of the spoil. "We cannot carry it all home," they said to each other. "There is too much. It will take us days and days to stockpile this wondrous booty."

Now, child of God, it will be the same for you. I do not know how, but if you can only trust God and praise Him and go straight ahead, you will see such wondrous things that you will be utterly astonished.

They Returned Singing

Then what will you do? Why, you will at once begin praising the Lord, for that is what the Israelites did. They went home singing. *"They came to Jerusalem, with stringed instruments and harps and trumpets, to the house of the LORD"* (2 Chron. 20:28). When God has done great things for you and brought you through your present difficulty, you must be sure to repay Him in the courts of His house with your loudest music and your most exultant notes, blessing again and again the name of the Lord.

They Rested in Quietness

After that, they had to rest. In the narrative it is added, *"Then the realm of Jehoshaphat was quiet, for his God gave him rest all around"* (2 Chron. 20:30). Their enemies were afraid to come and touch them any more. After a very harsh storm, it generally happens that there is a long rest. So will it be with all the Lord's people. You will get through this trouble, friend, and afterwards it will be smooth sailing for a very long time.

I have known a child of God who faced a cyclonic experience; it seemed as if he would be utterly destroyed. But after it was over, there was not a ripple on the calm of his life. People have envied him and wondered at his quietness. He had had all his storms at once, and when they were over, he came into smooth water that seemed unruffled.

Perhaps you will have the same experience. Ask the great Pilot of the Galilean lake to steer you safely through your tempest, and then, when the storm ceases at His bidding, you will be glad because you can be quiet. He will bring you to your desired haven.

I have desired to speak these comforting words to God's children, for well I know how you are tried, and I pray that the Lord, the Comforter, will apply these words to your troubled hearts.

But I never can finish my writing without having the very sad thought that there are always some to whom these comforting truths do not apply. They are not believers. They have never trusted in Christ. If this is so with you, my friend, you have to fight your own battles. You have to bear your own trials. You have to carry your own burdens, and when you come to the last great Day and stand before the judgment seat, you will have to answer for your own sins and bear your own punishment.

May God have mercy on you and deliver you from such a condition as this. It is a bad condition to live in. It is a terrible condition to die in. May you receive Christ as your substitute and your surety and glorify His name forever and ever.